T0160591

by John Yau

Poetry and Prose

Crossing Canal Street (1976)
The Reading of an Ever-Changing Tale (1977)
Sometimes (1979)
The Sleepless Night of Eugene Delacroix (1980)
Notarikon (1981)
    (with drawings by Jake Berthot)
Broken Off by the Music (1981)
Corpse and Mirror (1983)
Dragon's Blood (1989)
    (with drawings by Toni Grand)
Radiant Silhouette: New & Selected Work 1974–1988 (1989)
Big City Primer: Reading New York at the End of the Twentieth Century (1991)
    (photographs by Bill Barrette)
Giant Wall (1991)
    (with etchings by Jurgen Partenheimer)
Flee Advice (1991)
    (with drawings by Suzanne McClelland)
Postcards from Trakl (1992)
    (with etchings by Bill Jensen)
Genghis Chan: Private Eye (forthcoming)
    (with lithographs by Ed Paschke)
Edificio Sayonara (1992)

Monographs

Forrest Bess (1988)
Brice Marden: A Vision of the Unsayable (1988)
Don Van Vliet (1991)
Miguel Angel Rios (1991)
Nicola De Maria (1992)
A. R. Penck (forthcoming)

Editor

The Collected Poems of Fairfield Porter (1985)
    (with David Kermani)

JOHN YAU

EDIFICIO

SAYONARA

BLACK SPARROW PRESS · SANTA ROSA · 1992

ACKNOWLEDGMENTS

Poems have appeared in the following magazines: *American Poetry Review, Contemporanea, Grand Street, Hambone, Kaimana, Lacanian Ink, Lift, Oblek, Paris Review, Talisman,* and *The World.*

Grateful acknowledgment is also made to Timken Publishers for its use of "Western Rectangle" in *Big City Primer: Reading New York at the End of the Twentieth Century* (in collaboration with Bill Barrette); to Laura Carpenter Fine Art for its use of "Angel Atrapado VII" (Titled "Angel Atrapado") in the catalogue, *Joan Mitchell: Trees and other paintings 1960 to 1990*; to Galleria Communale d'Arte Moderna, Villa delle Rose, for its use of "The Invisible Painting Comes to Light" in the catalogue, *Ontani*; to Lehigh University Art Galleries for its use of "Big Island Notebook" in the catalogue, *Drawings and Poetry* (in collaboration with Michael Kessler); to Twelvetrees Press for its use of "Album" in *Gods of Earth and Heaven* by Joel-Peter Witkin.

An earlier version of the sequence, *Giant Wall: A Notebook,* was published as *Giant Wall* by Hine Editions, Limestone Press, in a limited edition with etchings by Jürgen Partenheimer.

The sequence, *Postcards from Trakl,* was published by Universal Limited Art Editions (ULAE) in a limited edition with etchings by Bill Jensen.

I would also like to thank the following editors for their support: Lynn Crawford, Joe Donahue, Ed Foster, Peter Gizzi, Nathaniel Mackey, Thomas McEvilley, Connell McGrath, Tony Quagliano, Eric Reiselbach, Patricia Storace, Lewis Warsh, and Arthur Vogelsang.

Black Sparrow Press books are printed on acid-free paper.

LIBRARY OF CONGRESS CATALOGING-IN-PUBLICATION DATA

Yau, John, 1950-
  Edificio Sayonara / John Yau.
    p.   cm.
  ISBN 0-87685-888-4 (cloth) : $25.00. — ISBN 0-87685-887-6 (pbk.) : $12.50. — ISBN 0-87685-889-2 (signed cloth) : $30.00
    I. Title.
PS3575.A9E3   1992
811'.54—dc20   92-33090
                                                                    CIP

Table of Contents

III. BIG ISLAND NOTEBOOK

IV. GENGHIS CHAN: PRIVATE EYE

V. POSTCARDS FROM TRAKL

VI. TWO SERIES

Edificio Sayonara

I

ODES

Proscenium

The wires in his head were leaking
juice spurted down his occipital ridges

He had left his footprints in an envelope on the desk
and couldn't find his way out of the sentences

charging towards him, their yellow headlights
washed in the prose of secondary emotions

Version A: She wrote the letter but did not mail it
Version B: She remembered the question years later

when she saw someone looking at her
from the ledge below

There is the woman who cured herself
the man who cured others

on the avenue behind the bushes near the trees
I (or someone who took my name)

entered the stadium where antique cars
were piloted by amnesiacs in yellow hats

This was seen daily in Milan
a chorus of twelve women in blackface

dancing, playing banjos, and singing
Stephen Foster songs in Italian

A woman boils her radio
squeezes the skids out of her nails

The general admires himself in the mirror
his moustache the envy of his entire staff

Three men in stained laboratory coats
discuss the events which led them

to an old hotel
on the outskirts of the empire

The first man begins: My mother
garbled the transmission

The second whispers: My parents
are a fiction conceived of by someone

who knew how to paint an official portrait
The third tells the others

that his partner is a woman
who speaks about herself in the fourth person

The steel zeroes of last night's conversation stubbed the air
Version C: A young girl trimmed her wishes to fit the
          occasion

while her mother listened with government trained ears
There is the tale of the photograph sent to Portugal

and the phonecalls that ensued
There are the precious nuggets

and the instructions anyone can follow
models of smoke and empty wrappers

There is the version in which none of this happens
and the audience is content to know

everything turned out as planned

First Ode to My Desk

(for Clark Coolidge)

The first square measuring time is a troublesome state of affairs. A succession of public enemies and secret members passes through chewed lead without significant seizures of color. Trees no longer speak. Ink stops in single plastic vein pointing down toward frozen planet. Only ripple in city drumbeat from the warehouse below, thoughts wrapped and packaged, voice of the salesman as he measures your interior dimensions, auditorium in which a line of light is projected onto the wall.

I read it wrong, and the phrase—"stars of the book"—slipped off the tiled sky. Pink clouds rose above crevices, membranes and fish bones fastened to the sun. Suppressed blot, funded castle, exact permission. I heard thought's passing but could not put it down fast enough to remember what it said before crumbling. I listened to traffic glued inside its own snarling desire to reach through a blouse, turn soft flesh into a body with no string unraveling from its circumference, a face pasted with posters.

This morning you tried to retrieve the one or two words sticking to the roof of the page, numbered bunk you circled, featherless and hunkered down against dry winds. Oh, drive off it. There are lots of things you can say. Machines will soon be humming, and many unused hours are waiting in the penthouse of detention. You live here and cannot visit them. You rent a leaf outside the walls and cannot move away from the neighborhood.

Perhaps this is the moment when the babble, its lapidary soap, yields to the music inside the phone. I sew my mouth shut. I place my head on the end of a spear and throw it through the door. No one knocks.

Second Ode to My Desk

Hours adrift beside an empty cockpit
Square moon rising above mattress fizz
I kiss the prospects docking beneath
the marble citizens, lift fingers
against door softener, call others
draining the future of focused intelligence
I used to be shorter
I used to be able to carry a tune
from the well to the burning house

Third Ode to My Desk

So that dinner consisted of
four people seated
around a wooden rectangle
husband wife two sons

And each was a dot on a map
a city steaming with alleyways
children lifting their cups
towards the crowds rushing past

So that dinner consisted of
a husband, a wife, and two sons
swallowing their words carefully
so that nothing escaped their mouths

There were no roads
to connect these dots together
though they formed a square
dividing the rectangle into a star

So that the husband
sometimes talked
about what had happened to him
after he left the apartment or room

and when he saw
that no one was listening
replaced his story
with its identical twin

So that everyone nodded
like pigeons
strutting in the square of their city
picking at the food before them

So that today I am
bent over the desk
knowing this is as far
as the words will go

Fourth Ode to My Desk

The words circle back
catch you at the desk again

looking at and over
planes of floating names

Another illusion
of leaving the room

where someone
is waiting

to separate you
from your head

the one that speaks
when the other is silent

Fifth Ode to My Desk

Is
it
what
is
this
only
now

Now
only
this
is
what
it
is

Sixth Ode to My Desk

Today it is no more than an empty theater where small boys search the floorboards for corroded coins. A bareheaded man is standing at one end of the stage. After consulting the list of rumors he inherited from his father, he begins painting orgies on the sides of caskets. Some believe these are forgeries of a world that never existed, while others remember the morning the river set out towards the sea never to return.

Since the surface layers of the soil prevent them from scaling great heights, the monkeys have decided to vote on whether the statue of a general is holding a scepter or a banana above his head. Veterinary work has been neglected and once again portions of their brain have fallen into disrepute.

I have never been fond of the arduous life of a cultivator.
I prefer lying to my flocks and herds.
I disdain trading of any sort.

II
G I A N T   W A L L   (A Notebook)

Black plates dipped into the sky
their mirrors collecting starlight
and sending it to other mirrors
fragments suspended
inside glistening velocities
their clusters of sounds rippling
toward the capital of tongues
Bubbles along the fringes of a shifting night
Acceptable parameters in which "he" is an illlusion
a particle pronoun seated at a table
stringing the spaces between words together
accumulating evidence of what is floating behind the now
setting out toward the rooms of the visible

There is no there to get to
no platform by the side of the way station
adjacent to the now in motion
All now starting off from somewhere
Memories of events flowing out
to where you and I might be standing
looking up
seeing evidence of what was unfolding itself
Artifacts of that now passing through
the now we look back on
its inscriptions deflecting us toward
the signal rooms between the here and there

1

In his observatory, the architect of smoke
keeps track of the vines of infectious mirages
migrating from winter stars to autumn leaves
Dust's ghosts unfolding their wings
in the spaces above holes
in words without circumferences
moonlit parenthesis in which the now
is stalled between commas
and the poet's mattress is stuffed
with the other side of vehement rapture

2

In his observatory, the architect of smoke
asks: What if all entrances and exits are blocked
by the shadows you cast before you
bodies without substance
solid as the ice you inhabit
when there is no "you" to discover
no "I" that speaks in your name

Mind's door swings around itself
Room an axial shovel
tilted beneath and behind
prismatic shifts clenching
warehouses of sensory data
How to elevate receiver
beyond circuit board
of housebound blasphemies
bolting the eyes backward
How to get into the meanwhile
melting towards the now that has left

What about the pages behind the pages
What about the ones we have written
and lost, renamed and renumbered
What about the ones orbiting
above the dome of syllables we inhabit

Moon's black walls dipped in acid
its pebbled ceiling bubbling through
the pages folded between stars

Beyond the optic curve
a bucket drops down
gathers foam from stars
lit by the ice within their vast aparts
The sky's walls are wind
and their windows thoughts
speared by squirms of light

October night opens
its book of leaves above leaves

Spoked pinwheel rolls against
last stars to reach house on hill

I am walking out
to meet myself returning

from where I have never been
nearer to where I am standing

my hands on the sky

Stars flicker
vaporous pixels set adrift, segments and substitutes
names given to clusters, nouns arranged in sequence
syllables formed along ridges, branches, and cores—
the stately unfolding going and returning
occasional paroxysms, call them shivers, swirling up
through layers and crusts, this is known to occur
somewhere remote from all metaphors, taut nets trembling
as residue is gathered out of celestial filaments
thrown into books, pages sifted and burned
words rising in parallel signals
clouds published in molten derivatives
ink running down sides hidden from all strata
ink collecting in jars under shelves of air
under skies filling with fossils dug up and displayed
under other names waiting beyond peripheries of speech

Words or images or what detonates them
when they no longer point to the events they name
their trajectories splitting the sky implanted in his cranial orbit.

The Mayan blood donor reads his horoscope
the arsonist of museums unrolls a cigarette
the robot of computer waste fiddles with its tie
beneath the rotation of stars
projecting their strings
down into mind's snowdrifts
Night emptied of all signs of you
its particles of smoke and air
released from the mirror of pronouns
And still the desire to enclose expands

Polar storms drift across notebook night
Ancient eyes once pinned syllables
to strings and wheels dangling from sky's mouth

I have a thirst to reach what is around
an imaginary corner
Dog fabric swelling with breasts of smoke

You told me
you would draw the doorway in which we had been standing,
looking over our shoulders at the words drying behind the sky.

We were ashes in a cave, dancing beneath night's cold fire.

42

Black dust
Surrogate tongue or brush

(call it asteroid interference
or somatic clot)

disperses into the atmosphere
Call them particles or embers,

last remains
or first inkling of words

by which you might come to know
exactly where you are standing

walking on earth's shifting shelves
a half-written book

some pages missing
others eaten by mice

slipping through the door
linking this now to any other

A
new
planet
gleams
in
its
puddle
of
ink

Water
fills
the
basin
with
light
from
distant
stars

III

BIG ISLAND NOTEBOOK

Papoa Inoa

I bought it in a bookstore on Kona,
read a few pages on the plane from Kona

to Honolulu, put it down on the plane
from Honolulu to Los Angeles,

and, later, handed it to you on the flight
between Los Angeles and New York

I thought it would fill the time I was in the air
between one named place and another

Now it is in the knapsack on the seat beside me,
air conditioned bus from Manhattan to Morristown

Long stiff bristles from the raffia palm
Diamonds in the alluvial gravel

Didn't one of my professors say "travel equals trade"
twenty years ago in a 19th century mansion

overlooking the Hudson
The Society of Kastorians is on Sixth Avenue

above a newly renovated delicatessen
Billiards, billiares, biglitardo

Tony pallet, utility wonder
Pay money at the gate

If none of our presidents has had a good doctor
what are we to expect

The author is lying in a display case
Traffic and weather go together

She carries a chair with her
whenever she leaves the apartment

Valley Fair (a store)
Fair Valley (a novel

written by a disgruntled gentleman
living in Galway)

You can press his pants
but you cannot pant

when he presses you
against his Tuscan postcards

Union Millburn Shiloh Antietam
Two big deposits have been discovered,

and at the time of writing
a decision still has to be reached

on which will be worked first
Her leg is on fire

48

Mouth partly open,
portion of pink tongue showing

They lie on a bench
outside the railway station

African tulips beside garbage truck
parked in front of church

Summit Chatham Madison Morristown
New eyes for the needy

How do you detail your car
Have liberty will travel

Turn down Middle Avenue
Blunt-headed funeral danglers

Phones for phonies
Three chickens crossed the road

Yellow school bus, children
gathered in the gazebo

The old neck speaks
Joys of evolution

Each morning he would walk
the length of the beach

swinging a metal detector
Bugs Bunny's birthday

Right lane must spawn blight
What kind of hair tonic does he use

Franklin and Myrtle
Frankincense and myrrh

Woman with cast in blue sling
(Cross out) moving cartons

The little balloons (all blank)
above Nancy and Sluggo

Hill and Elm
Purple skirt suspenders white knit pullover

Brick wall chain link fence with barbed wire
along the top, untrimmed hedge

Arm technology headquarters
Do not write until you see the wires in their eyes

I bought her an answering machine
She gave me a suitcase

No wonder it's not working
I am learning to read the instructions

Look for jewels in the toad's head
The dial turns toward

one end of the century
filling the air with neon light

Big Island Notebook 1

I read you a story and then I become a character in it.
It is a cold red evening, and the day's fish are drying
in the windows facing the future. I am lost and must
begin interpreting the yellow hexagons stenciled with
black silhouettes (one donkey on fire, one man with an
arrow rising from his back, two overturned milk bottles),
if I am to leave this cobblestone plateau behind. You tell me
I have to reach the author of these sentences before his hand
chisels a new set of words into our foreheads. The wind shifts
from one jurisdiction to another.

I am standing beneath a billboard, waiting for you to add up
the empty skies between us.

Big Island Notebook 2

The faucets release their tepid streams of rust. It is dawn, and you are standing beside me, brushing your teeth. A film erupts across the mirror we use to broadcast and receive our images, their perforated fans. There are a large number of crates with the word "column" stenciled on the wooden side. Next to each one is a carefully rendered line drawing of two men playing cards. You finish your morning rituals and leave the room, but I do not know if it is the one I am seeing or the one I am standing in. At least the men know who is on the other side, you sing from the adjacent square, its edges bristling with smoke.

Big Island Notebook 3

I am wondering why I am wearing a raincoat and realize it is cold and damp. We are standing in a jail cell full of bright yellow birds. You say I thought they were extinct. Hundreds of years ago, people living on the island we are about to visit captured them for their feathers. Does this make us extinct? I whisper. Why do you call them verbs when they can no longer fly toward the trees outside these walls? you ask. I cannot answer. I cannot tell if my mouth is full of feathers or sand. You tell me that I have achieved a state bordering on happiness, closer to it than to the concrete floor beneath our feet. After all, you have only two conclusions to choose from. And each of them will open a door to one of the rooms hidden inside the images separating you from speech.

In the photographs I am wearing a green bathing suit. The woman I am embracing is sporting a blue bikini. You tell me she is a statue reflecting light, the lumpy matter that emerged from a mold. See how the skin glistens under the glare of the camera, its single eye focused on the little quiver of air between the two of you. I ask, where were you when this thimble of air was pocketed? Behind the mirror, you answer. An image cannot be remembered if there is no slab on which to mount it. In this case there are three slabs: you, her, and now this.

Big Island Notebook 5

I burned the letter, but kept the ashes in a jar beside the bed. Flowers bloomed beneath the moon, flimsy sickles of color separating the wind into dried insect wings, each wrinkled and ready to use. Then you came out of the shower, a towel wrapped around your favorite mirage. Are we ready to send and receive each other's images?

I am lying beneath the chandelier wondering if I can become a mirror catching your flight. Or have you come to the end of the sentences that brought you here? The words spill beyond their contours. I was looking for a branch library, you reply, while you were praising buckets of resin flowing from a paper sky.

You spent the morning walking around an island hidden
on this island, a refuge for flowers that cannot grow
anywhere else. In the garden there are petals that
shine and ones that smell. There is the Mickey Mouse
plant and the tree named after one of the Seven Dwarfs.
According to the brochure, the names are an added
attraction, something to remind us of our childhood.
You told the guide that between the garden of names,
what he called "childhood," and your memory of it, there
are any number of pages. Some of them lit by the moon,
others dangling from the stars. When he could draw you
a map that showed you where those flowers were growing,
you would begin believing that "childhood" was a word
everyone could share.

Big Island Notebook 7

We wanted to pass through the tunnel without smelling the urine, buy thick red rectangles for dinner. We entered a sequence surrounded by other sequences (call them sentences without direction, you whisper). Nature's flaws were oozing out of the sky. Burning funds grazed my feet and face, smoke unraveled your shadow's blue sweater. What will it be like when we reach the remnants of yesterday's weather? I ask. This is not the time to begin speculating. We must stick to the sentences we assigned ourselves, the ones fleeing the muse of representation.

I put my head and favorite hat in a paper bag, carry them down to the jewelry store where you are working. There is nothing I can recommend, you tell me. A ring is too small and a necklace too large. Perhaps you should return it to its rightful owner, the one who let you take it down from the shelf and pretend it was yours. I plead innocent as I skip out the door, knowing that I will miss the moment you begin unbuttoning your blouse. The sky turns its pages, and I walk faster, trying to stay inside the chapters no one has ever remembered reading. This way, I hear you screaming. You must go this way or else the night will shovel you back into its mouth of bright, oily stars.

The tour of the copper mines ended without warning, and the bus turned back toward the pink hotel. You were afraid you had told me too much about the moments when you felt invisible. I think I only know how to make a present of myself, deliver it to others so that their hands might unwrap the bandages. Alligator nylons and zebra skin underwear are very popular this year. I was listening to you speak, your voice rising and falling into a whisper. The windows were dirty streaks, remnants of a landscape turning to dust and water. We were careening down a mountain road, and our driver was singing to the angels waiting for us just up ahead. I wanted to point to the birds rising from the yellow fields, the clouds molting. But you were telling me about the bandages, about how they were not bandages but something else. And did I know what you meant. And how could I, having never been inside the world from which you just emerged.

After hunting all morning, the troopers enter the commissary and begin looking for deodorant. I am in the aisle of promises, while you are humming a song of repair. Later, in the dark, we dwindle into two strings, staring at the ceiling. You turn and whisper: Perhaps the next time I will etch my lips with roses. We could draw each other's portrait in blood, I answer (thinking I have outsmarted you in this game of descent). But you don't know how to draw, you answer. Besides, what shall we use for paper? And who will go first?

We swerved to avoid the soap memory places at the intersection of each of our infractions against the vocabulary we choose to continue our discussion, knowing in advance that one of us might flip onto his or her back, lie like a beetle beneath the animal sun.

You ask. What words will return us to the words we were using yesterday? The ones that were red and green and wore us inside, their cowls softening the blasts (call them: letters to the interior, double catechism, or windy night)?

Instead of answering, I tell you that I have decided to return my hands to their owners, and begin packing for the journey to the bus station. It is not so easy to give certain parts away, you warn. And yes, I too will stop standing between myself and the sight of my body walking into the painting of fire. Maybe once we have run out of ways to fill the air between us, the air will point to our places on the page, the stick figures who have just emerged from the caves, tears running down their hands, smoke curling through the crumbling membrane.

You return from your encounters with the other side of the page. I hear you in your room, shoes dropping to the floor, closets opening and closing, the shuffling of voices until you find the one pinned to an uninfected broadcast band. I stand outside your door and pretend to be skipping stones across the lake or night we still have to cross, its glassy surface another of history's deceptions. I hear someone singing and think it is you. The wind has closed the book, you announce, and crushed us between its silvery lies. The illusion of triumph has mastered us again. Tonight, we will go out and watch the children slip out of one game and into another.

And closer to home, the ants have erected a fort without telling us the password.

Tropical Bulbs 1

In a village huddled along a steep margin, an agent shows
up and counts the sounds missing from the children's
tongues. He makes a list and hands it to the oldest inhabitant
who can still read without the aid of glasses.

*Red is for the channel through which the waters flow; yellow
is an obstacle, a skunk or stone; green is an extension of a foul
scheme; add black, subtract two blues, and you will have your
answer.*

Inoculated sky, a long broken hill of clouds, caravans
of disease ploughing across the highway. Behind the
clay flats stands the remnants of a temple, an open air
market, a hotel, and a pyramid marking the tomb of the
diesel train. Each mound is surrounded by a bare patch
and shows up in an aerial photograph as a dense rash
of white dots.

The older warriors swim beneath their granite bosses,
rising only to consume plant and animal remains. The
younger ones perform functions comparable to their
tattooed adversaries. Others hide inside the theaters that
helped dispose of the larger animals that once roamed
the unlit streets leading to the harbor.

A uniformed man collects gum from beneath the chairs and ships it to pasture lands traversing the plains. A row of mouths is pressed against the glass, lips wet and eyes moist. He is lying on the floor and asking her to arrange his limbs in all the positions required by the questionnaire. Their answers provoke subsidies from those who sit on the other side of the window, taking bets and waiting for the action to begin.

She remembers the first time she unbuttoned her blouse inside an elevator. They were between drinks named after emperors who slithered across cool marble floors. She thought he was whispering the letters of something that was floating inside his pants. It was nearly spring. Rain had started trickling through the cracks in their plan.

Tropical Bulbs 2

He called her Persian Storm, White Island Peace, Turtle Clown,
and Beloved Fiend. She was in the other mansion, sucking up
moisture, turning into an epitaph of tires rolling over his
liberty goblets.

The agate twins melted their wings behind a row of busted
neon spheres. Drenched in the cheapest planets of wealth,
the pimply faced wind was busy bestowing martyrs on
the towers where the necessary chemicals were stored.
A Greek elegiast listed the powders, their power, according
to the minerals in which they had been boiled.

We preserve the names of our commodities in the names we
give our children. We use these branches of knowledge to
wean our citizens away from their dependence on the residual
deposits locked inside airport hangars, their vermillion veins
infiltrating the lists, grottoes of excess where flowers
without clothes live inside our toys.

I dubbed his inventions, their lazy seeds and spindles of white
breath, while he became entangled in the pills of his master,
her stout birds pecking at the land of stars and spices. Thus my
eyes fed on the hush of their mountains, the languages they
invented before the mirror of music pouring from their lies.

We walk past the cemetery of crocodiles, turn and enter the
quarry, its banks of waste and unfinished columns of figures
rising from the rugs of another dynasty. I belong to one of the
lesser procession, a carrier of flasks or the janitor who
sweeps dust from the nomads passing through. You trace
your shadow in the mud, wait for it to harden into a funnel
of light projected above our heads.

Blue smoke rises toward the stars painted on the ceiling.

A woman unbuttons the mist clinging to her lips.

Volcano Park

Stings fill the windows. Yellow with insect saliva. Porous black stones (they look like cheese from another planet) accumulate below a postcard bucket interrupted by fluffy splashes. Tornadoes of ants rise to the surface of a fruit strewn field. Queequeg, Joe Kahahawai, and Edward Louie are parked in a truck outside the Dodo Mortuary.

Lugged, logged, lagged. Mimosa blue marble cigar box. Serrated funicular throb marks off its circle. Hula-headed skinks clamber over the transom. Burnt toast hair, popcorn eyes.

Oh hail, all palooka muck. May I kill a kin with a pale ukelele? A Meek howl in napkin clank. Cone hop on a hula noon. Wake a kick. Papal pannikin. Wall pock malm. Kinky kimono. Mock palm wall. Open nylon melee. Puny walloon kiwi. Why pack wallop in a clap mill?

Cool agile teardrop. Ornate pyramid saddle. Juvenile raccoon thread. Oval zebra snowflake. Sergeant peacock cleaner.

Logical traffic glide. Twist dials and peer through periscope of an antique radio, its amber porthole and pearl chants. Listen to Robert Louis Stevenson, Mark Twain, and Jack London boil shrimp beneath the banyan trees. Reach for the chrome banana.

We are going to have to mongoose it out of him, hold his blue tongue up to the light. Does he expect the dumb in me to illuminate the coral in him? The discovery of salvageable children beneath the burlesque hall arouses little attention among the tutors of leather and latches.

Midnight's terrace planted with silver leaves. Sanctified field crammed with chiseled statistics. Crone office building, rollaway with rocks. Palomino worms scrawl left cleavage. The villagers have no pornographer, but the mayor has started writing to see if there is a painter who will journey to the edge of the earthquake district. If he fails to satisfy their curiosity, they will dismember him, and use his hands as flyswatters.

Lapis neon scalloped lava shelves. Floppy butterfly devotees.

Pope Geronimo the Innocent.

The song survives because a man is bitten by one of the dogs taking apart the dance.

Feathers, shells, and human hair.

Muy pukka bella.

Western Rectangle

North of the factory outlet tall grasses predominate, with large gnarled trees near the main generator and at the base of old termite mounds. The remaining rivers have faded back into the map, leaving teams of miners to look for another way to haul food to the surface. Stolid faces, bodies lacking the raw materials. Industrial promises unfulfilled throughout the long season of fixed prices and sectioned families.

The older men have worked in a shoe factory, a sled assembly plant, a lever complex, and a clothing dump. The blast buttons neither diminished the barriers nor altered the direction of their sickness. Some will live long enough to decode the blur of pages in their hand.

Under a tunnel of gray light, she unbuttons her blouse, holds her breasts up to the face hidden in the movie theatre. A huge lidless eye looks down and sees only its own shadow beneath the streetlamp, a woman untying her scarf, a moment's bubble leached of all its colors. He tells her her name, the size of the kiss she left inside him when he was shoveling snow through the window of another era. They met before a deceitful story, read the words stenciled on the gleaming sky. The next chapter sends its signal, frozen and punctuated. Some other dance, he thinks. Some other crime, she replies.

I enter the recycling zone, try inhabiting the mind's available space. Something must be done to retrieve the books floating above the dust. I remove windows, walls, and door. I cope with the climate, the many pests it develops in pockmarked gamblers. Sixty years ago Manhattan was nothing more than a campsite overlooking hundreds of corrals. Pastoralists roamed through the open countryside, looking for evidence of communication from the boreholes.

IV

GENGHIS CHAN: PRIVATE EYE

Genghis Chan: Private Eye VIII

I plugged in the new image fertilizer
and complained to my inaudible copy

We did tour the best spots
trying to attract basic signs of pity

touched a disaster every now and then
and remained ridiculous and understaffed

Now I am clamped to the desk
unraveling thought's stunted projectiles

Had I been as visible as a chameleon
I would have crossed my eyes

so as to look more like you
than your silver reflection

I would have hummed to the statue
inside your black eyes and black tongue

I would have memorized its song

Genghis Chan: Private Eye IX

I was headed toward a surprise I could not return,
its twisted little forehead and clinging grin
waiting beside the fountain of cakes.

Who dropped the water-bearing rocks
through the mail slot? Why does the moon
admire the rich, their diamond curls

glassine beneath bags of yellow dust?
Why does the sky carry its entrails around?
I was babbling before I started,

my mouth glued to the lips
floating above monkey clouds.
Foam spilled from its huddle of frozen intentions,

each drop armed with an emblem.
Lucky, no gun is glistening
beside the puddles drifting down Happy Avenue.

Genghis Chan: Private Eye X

Wine steeped clouds
ignite city's rim

Bubbles float up
to roof of mouth

burst into clods
spooning wooden crumbs

from reptile reruns
I ride notes down

stick scratching
dirt walls

axis blurt
and scrawny rabble

watch indelible water
seep through clocks

Genghis Chan: Private Eye XI

Small hunks drift
tumble across their shoes

Porous metal scrapes
top rung of hired dreamers

Surrounded by clumped tongues
fenced-out eyes

Insistent paddle drifter
Smeller of candies

I patrol the mattress stained windows
twiddle down hours

until the next shifter releases me
from my solemn valves

A service examiner of bodies
pumped into the last lanes of alley grass

I keep my head in my lap
and train small turtles to cry

I am a piece of cake
stacked against the company wall

Genghis Chan: Private Eye XII

The apology corpses watch
little matchsticks of wit

illuminate the park
Slender stalks are goosed

from their tripods
mounted on

chubby dinner plates
I am outside of

the helium conference
hopping from grunt to grunt

A battered jabberer
launches his coffee

streams out his arms
whispers

I received my certificate
to practice being humus

I too am a yellow lamp
bolted to the elephant sky

77

Genghis Chan: Private Eye XIII

It's hard to keep pretending
you're a dusty chink
in a hall of yellow linen

You begin believing
you're just another handkerchief
wiping away the laundresses' tears

Genghis Chan: Private Eye XIV

My new yellow name
was ladled over

your installment plan
Another blue dollar special

bubbling below
the Avenue of Ovens

used star slots
and their three laces

A bomb in a raincoat
was inserted later

Shell or shill
Black pills to slip

the old horse down
I was fired on slanted legs

copying your words
onto matches and axes

as if they were gods
with wooden bellies

Genghis Chan: Private Eye XV

You broke the star
I pinned to the ceiling

that stacked sky
I swam beneath

toward the window
where you were landing

watching a yellow moonlit
race of bold potatoes

outrunning the new elite
the stain clingers and honey babble

You were a music taker
at home in the spit

Genghis Chan: Private Eye XVI

Another mule in the spoon trade
among the pigeon rankers
of the slowest crank
I danced among
the fossil bunglers
and gelatinous geezers

A crutch program
gone soft in the lead
slithering up the pegs
I imitated others
leading to the ladder of sighs

Genghis Chan: Private Eye XVII

I was the wood doctor
who made mouse calls

pluck for more
I stuffed bullet boxes

with yellow jelly snacks
and counted raked lumps

from the neck of my bruise
I was a name staller

heisting scalped hearts
a golden waged

hardware jolter
in blue stuffers

wallowing daintily
in the mutt routine

when I was bleached beneath
the bend of my last sale

Genghis Chan: Private Eye XVIII

Follow the pimple instructions
You're supposed to

splash them down
scream side first

Spot a diamond
mooch peddler

stalking his puddle
to the corner number

the wrist of occupations
swindling the best drams

from her flaccid rustle
Steam out a defective colonel

selecting moles to hoist
beside a fellow sled buoy

Store the verbs
of a rock making

mock raker
stilled by the smiles

of easy soot
sifting his pay

Grease the tines
of every genuine article

transmitting
radio wives

through the granular flight
Spill the inventory of stars

we sold to the voices
stained above our beds

Genghis Chan: Private Eye XIX

My stamped mother
used to fling to me

All stones lead to home
Go easy on the turtle pie

gored down
at doom temperature

Cast a cold
and dirty style

on every yellow
leaf of lassitude

glistening beneath
the grappled fly

My stamped mother
used to fling me

and I
her lump of muck

would fling back
all the riveted bones

I could dandle
on my wasted plea

the chink of meat
we knew that linked us

to the junk
going by

Genghis Chan: Private Eye XX

I posed
as a cookie
fortune smeller

I sold
the stale delays
your parents pranced to

the old bunch
gathered beside
the evening stalk

I squeezed
the liars alive

I bent their bubbles
around air's broken coat

V

POSTCARDS FROM TRAKL

Postcard 1

Rotary wind machines bend our words in half

Black steam erupts from the horizon

The ones whose bodies we jettisoned
on underground platforms
continue to call out

We have done what we were told
We have eaten dirt and stones
We have chopped ice and snow
into houses of praying dogs

Why can't one of us
be the choirmaster
who glues pebbles
to the bottom of everybody's tongue

Postcard 2

I will memorize the lessons
and deliver the gifts

A stern oaf
who goes boating

in the ebony spray
I will grow stale

a blue mutterer
who rolls through

lanes and ditches
I will count

the huts of red decay
their hallways and hecklers

In each thing I do
I will repeat

the illusion of being
a brainwashed man

burning alive
at his dual controls

Postcard 3

(Blue Movie)

Mudguard music
Gauze twilight shadow detection
Languid nylon airlift
Spore studded breath clogs departure points
Needy tenant caresses hidden laughter sheds
Porcupine motion unzipped
Immaculate star station hookup
Gleaming jackal incision
Fluid exchange unit
Decipher pressed mobile inscriptions
Five tunnel probers reach crimson hunger purse
Dark chambered plant of mouth soldered to windpipe
New version of two preserved reptile flashers

Postcard 4

(Blue Movie)

Every deadline is directed toward
red moon's last popular front

Wet hands and white dust
trace remaining contours

Memoirs of Egyptian cigarettes
hotel rooms and ankle bracelets

Dazed lungers go by
their plastic tails askew

Pencil brawls
long hours carhorn night

Swollen blue flame lips
sweep away stemmed tide

Postcard 5

(Imaginary Photograph)

You are a billiard ball
falling out of a newspaper

Two cranes are peeled off
the rear axle

Another head floats above a fish bowl
crammed with handcuffs and salt

The movie hut lounge
burns to a yellowed frown

An insolent sickness overtakes the student of gases
The skin of the tower is washed with lice

Postcard 6

Adolf Loos strangled glass birds
on the boardwalk of Tuxedo Park

Noon simmered in oval blue mirrors
mounted above strutting throngs

Our tour guide told us
there is a pavement or payment

that outlasts the stun of what occurs
beside the crimson river bed

Remember, tiny tastes of the new fatigue
are carefully measured out

No one cared to argue with the smoke
rising past our wax shoulders

Postcard 7

He lay beneath his pine cone bed,
a sensitive slab any shifting wind
could scrape or sink further
It was the moon he fished,
its pale blue echo, its vowels
drifting above the fuzzy swarm

This is sleep he said
its cold pillow and icy lips
were above or beside him
This is the crimson wall I have flopped beside
the ashes of another burned book

Postcard 8

(Dear Rilke)

Your tight lipped zoomers
have no bodies, while mine
have neither light nor air

Where is the dye or candle
we can bracket, castle
or boat we can cling to

Can I steal your ventriloquist gambler
Can you rescue a muddy foot soldier
and his box of salt

Postcard 9

Day's golden hearse drives past
Another miner will soon be lost
in a cloak of blaring wolves

Postcard 10

Today's forecast: Ash tendrils
will continue sprouting
from the spigots of your brass radio

Postcard 11

Radiant wreckage

plugs its pendulum
above a school bus

Another pirate wind
enlists the nudes

printing their breasts
against the pond

Bees probe my
metal forehead

Yes, I am still carrying
your beak in my mouth

Postcard 12

I am a row of golden diesel tags
under altered elms

I am a day's earnings
when the day eludes me

I am a blue spiel
slumming in Leipzig

a denim mind
versed in rosy sewage

I am a gutter skirt
or a skirted gutter

a fiery herd
whose profile

is set against
walled hymns

I want to sink
in callow moans

I want to strip
the greasy donut gangs

of all their golden cares

I collect tolls from rocks
antlers from men

I tell myself
I am sipping

from a bowl of green sherbert
while flags dance lazily

before our catcalls
I wake up

knife my face
from the ice

watch smoke
rise from the lake

You are beside me
untying your hair

Your neck is starting to snow

Postcard 14

She is talking to the bread again, saying the little things
that will make it turn its battered head back to the clock,
its dish of erased eggs. The eldest son counts craters, takes
photographs of tears coalescing around his sister's eyes,
while the youngest son cannot remember when he noticed
the words carved into his skin, the list of idols whose names
he will someday be old enough to learn.

She walked down the hallway,
opened the door
and entered

the side of the world
I had just left
In The House of Stare

words are pins and thimbles
Children crawl into their books
sleep between the pages of smoke

rising from their foreheads
I counted the letters of her name
as if they would lead me

to the minerals on which they were written
Cars stopped long enough
to make themselves heard

above their shiny debts
But didn't you try to remove
yourself from this story?

Yes, I took the trolley past the lake,
got out and stood beneath
the stunned blinks

And yes, I too
am a flaked piece
torn from a scab edition

Postcard 16

Memory's branch quivers
beneath the weight of a butterfly

How am I to know what it wants
without asking

Could it be that simple, the question
and then the answer

Why do we fall outside of these additions
or consult the zodiac surrounding us

read its rotten walls and bulb glare
Why substitute names for things

when the things name us
(our vowels and consonants)

into their sleep
one from which they will never awaken

Am I just an echo drifting back to myself
who is sitting beneath the river

drinking air
Something must have told me to say this

A rock or the memory of a rock
falling toward the shadow it once owned

Postcard 17

Blue and gold granite clouds
throng brain table of wires

and melting thoughts
lilt of one battery to another

Green and then yellow and green
in late afternoon flash of the span

reaching here to there
across the face of sagging days

not yet here, not yet stones
marking sod city streets

How long on this string between
two winds have I been wandering

never quite arriving
in one place in one piece

Postcard 18

The book closes its clocks on the poor
stranding them outside time's yellow factory

I used to count the stumblers and harridans
their feet and hands rising from the mud

I used to keep a diary of the jackets and shoes
I found beside the lighthouse

I used to point to the whistles
mounted above the city

the room of bank
or blank pages

the library we tried to open
Why skip into stories

you have been told
a child asked

or believe in the words
waiting on your doorstep

Conclusion A. I strolled beneath layers of ice
after vacuuming the dust off my voice

Conclusion B. I slipped between the slabs
and deposited the match in your hands

Postcard 19

The book delivers its message
across the ice floe

without understanding either the first
or second part of its command

I am here to count
the burned out bulbs

jammed in the rotting sky
I carry a load of face cream around

in a little pump
sewn inside the flaps of my lizard coat

My pronouns are waiting
for you and your husband

to kiss above the children buried in the lake
smile down at the faces smiling back

My pronouns are waiting
to be delivered to their proper slats

These words were written
on the ice of another star
before they were copied
onto the fields of this one

This patch of earth
we crawl in is a rotten fruit
and we are either its flies
or its managers

Postcard 21

When will the night
trust me and bring me
inside its silver bakery

When will the night
drop me from its blue antlers
and cavity of stiff fur

O when will the night
pour its nectar of illusions
through the stars in my forehead

A page burning
on the outskirts of

sky's broken gown
I will become

an uncertain memory
discharged from

clots of paint and air
or rust falling

from the clothes of a singer
who bathes his daughters

in yellow brine
I will live

to see myself
floating above

the Cemetery of Hours

VI

TWO SERIES

Avila 1

You learn to accomodate yourself to others, to fit into the
space left by their shadow. This is one way of disappearing
into the smile meant for the body you have left on the carpet,
where every rose is a perfect instrument of writing.

I saw myself swimming there, hidden behind the curtain some
call a face.

You can put it on hold, you tell yourself. You can lie until the
sun lifts itself out of your mouth. You can walk into the water
and not get wet.

We were in bed talking about lives lived, our lies and lovers.
The who how and where of what we had done during the years
we explored the outlying districts of a landscape almost
reaching the surface of our adopted skin. The breaths taken
and not taken, the words used to circle off a story, select its
gold plated dome, the dune it would ride into the sea.

I remember not wanting to get the couch dirty, it was brand
new, you said. Smiling. The rope of my desire reached a
balcony that could not be pictured except in the garage or
drive-in I drove past, blue top down all the way under the sky.
Black tray, newly mown stars. The buckled snug I laughed at.

119

I looked down into her green shoes. It was dawn, and I was hoping she had written her name there, in the gaps that held her feet when she walked around my twin, the one I carried with me whenever I wanted to see what I was doing. He was the dummy and I was the flutter passing through, on my way to a parking lot of iridescent kin.

Avila 2

I was not ready to buy the bathing suit she held up in front of her, like a welcome mat's incandescent mate. It was not always like this. Once I used to project myself into all the dimensions necessary to float above the mouth of tears bearing down on me, listen to the real story taking place inside the body I shared with my typewriter, its trees sticking to my skin. This picture was enough of a taste for them, the little ones that come neatly wrapped in cellophane lists and surplus skulls. I was a brick of prized allotment dancing above drying motors. A carriage of glass some took home and showed their mother. What they saw was a bucket. A page of the future burning inside an empty book.

Avila 3

How was I to know the one beneath me would become a fish,
a string of words rising from her mouth. How was I to know
she did not want to be all the things I could fit inside my
pillaged hands. But I was even smarter, and did as I was told.
I opened the mirror and stepped into the snow of history,
all it erases of the day we swim inside, upstream towards the
lights of a distant house. I began translating the tales of the
shadows and hats I encountered there: nomads with flashlights
riding their horses into the sea; women in shawls who only
cross the river beneath a half-eaten moon; the seizers and
sizzlers. I began believing in their tales, I began building
perfect pyramids beneath the sun.

Avila 4

I opened the mirror and stepped into a place where I could be a thing or an event but never both at once. Words slid off its page of ice, leaving me on a shelf overlooking the body other singers tried to inhabit. One day, I got up, left this city, its straw platforms and plaster windows, and walked east, towards the stars. I kept on walking, kept on telling myself that I would follow the words, that I would reach an oasis of dust, that I would drink its sweet air.

He kissed me beneath the wind and saw that no one was looking back. I was talking to myself, I told him. I was telling myself that there are steps to follow, maps to consult, and islands to visit. That some other story was being written on these lips and it wasn't mine to tell. He did not hear me because I had misplaced the address of the house I was visiting, a warm room beside a cool lake, red moonlight streaming past the door. He complimented me and I bowed, my shadow folding itself into a neat pile on the chair.

Give him this dance, I thought. Give him this and that step. It is the only extension he wants, the only one he can reserve.

Go outside and tell him the windows are open and the mirrors are clean.

Avila 6

I did not want volcano chumps illuminating the positions I had taken on the continental shelf. I did not want shadows staring down from ceilings of gray grease and open styrofoam cathedrals. I did not want hesitations to emerge from holiday corridors and yellow champagne glasses. But I was inside a book written in someone else's hand, turned this way and that by his lavish rifts of attention, the seances following a bedtime raffle. My words became mouthpieces, and a torn red peignoir, its slash of scarcity, stood up and spoke beneath the obedient moon, stars in the shape of forks. This is the number you wanted, I heard the dead sister of my only sister say, and this is the dance I know.

I began writing whatever came into my head, the one that looked down and saw you reaching across the table. I told you I had had it tested by someone I never met, someone who sent me postcards from faraway islands. You knew I was lying, and you agreed with my lie by acting as if you believed me.

You were standing on a chair looking for a way to lift up the ceiling and see the moon, its one remaining mitten soaked in brackish water. I told you to join me by the window. The sky and curtains trembled. My hand without rings and my hand with tiny cuts reached around you to learn if they could meet in the dark. Then it was dawn, and the sentences between the sentences were still empty. Little rooms with nothing written on the walls.

Each Other 1

In the middle of the unfolding, neither yours nor mine nor ours, simply one of many we are in, we occupy (*Read:* standing, sitting, sprawling) different quadrants of a room, waiting for night's air to open its pockets, let us slip into its cubbyholes of respite. This story is true in this room, but not in the tropical breeze outside the sentences spelling it out, neon pulses crashing against the cranial arena. You were speaking, though there is nothing to corroborate what I just heard, which was not you. I heard it nevertheless. We have reached the end of allegory, the thinking that makes this storytelling possible, and must now find a way to understand the space between us cannot be filled, that we are on different sides of a window that neither opens nor shuts.

Each Other 2

What you said filled me with an expectation I tried to eliminate, so as to hear what was actually coming toward me. The there in the now up ahead, its strings of warm blue lights wavering in the wind curling up out of the bay. I heard it because I was not (I thought) where it was, not in the room whose door had just been opened, but was where it could be once I took it in, like a picture whose boundaries remain intact in the indigo loam. I took it in, its music and its picture. It was not what you said, it was what I heard. *I crossed the Ganges in a balloon. It was during the time I was an envoy to the porridge of popular echoes.*

Each Other 3

You were crying and saying my name, but you weren't crying and what you were saying only resembled my name, a structure of echoing sound reverberating in the room simmering above the harbor. We breathe this water, always the slipping away is here to accompany us to separate places within the room, on the bed, by the window. Someone inside said jump or fly, that voice again, a lulling music sweeping up toward the sky's hot blue walls. You were telling a story to me and to yourself, words directed toward the time when you were small and fit into the hands of others, those that squeezed too tight and those that brushed themselves off. A story without room for either of us, a brick wall whose smooth surfaces invite tourists to stop and caress its ensemble, night when shame leaves such gestures intact as aspirins in a sealed bottle.

That air, its dust, was no longer available, no longer sold on counters dividing warehouses into displays, and we had to turn elsewhere to procure the necessary contraries. Talking, you said, is difficult when you are not sure who is talking and who is the one you think you are talking to, if indeed that is what you and I are doing. In the chronicle of resemblances even the rain becomes theoretical, and those whose mouths are filling with sand find it difficult to separate wall from sky, here from here. Once I told a man to take my shadow and find the body within. I knew I could not say this again and again without my body becoming level with the ground. I knew that what kept entering me I could neither keep nor expel, that they had become metaphors spinning within their own orbit. I still carry these orbits within, sometimes feeling them tugging me out to the edge of a day that has not occurred, or in towards a moment that slipped past, almost unnoticed until now.

Each Other 5

We melted into each other like snow. We crashed against each other like rocks. Neither accumulation held us within its orbit. I am between the here and the there, and I am trying to return to the moment of sunlight filling the doorway, where you are standing, looking at this form you think I always inhabit.

I had stopped believing there were other "I's" when we met, surprised myself by talking as if each of us was where we were, there in front of the other, nothing to hide or hide behind. The characters came later, the ones I am, the ones the others wanted to be, the ones arriving unannounced, speaking of the time we were in, the time they brought with them from the air of their own dreaming. To tell that story without being in it, theirs not mine. I thought I wanted to be the paper through which your story passes. I thought there was no other story to tell.

VII
ALBUM

Aduana

Register it rather than stand between it and this.
Pyramid face drifts sparkling in the cabbage
spilling down toilet trained mountains.
Two hands hold the boy high above the floor.
Men in ocher uniforms, the man who steps
out of the movie whose characters are cartoons
of the man stepping away from the screen,
pinned inside a story told by others.
This not that though that raises its umbrella
above this field of milling in the zone between,
on their way there. Somone always going,
the standard of expectations lowered by degrees,
mostly from college, and the air
filled with proper totes of dust.
He had been told the words were not his
even while they projected him into a place
where he could be seen, wearing the vocabulary
of one who is a microphone.

Chinese Landscape Above Caracas

The heavy gray and white clouds surrounding the dark green mountaintops reminded him of his grandfather. All the stories he had ever been told about him were lies. The hand that dipped the brush into the ink was not the one that guided its colors into stylized shapes and lines, each of which told a story about the window he was looking through when he decided to see the mountains, trees, and river. All the stories he listened to, as a child. The story he read the two children sitting on the trunk was make-believe. One made it to believe it. Who believes the stories that are being told is a child. Each story believes in itself.

The Painter Asks

(for Brice Marden)

Why go toward the palaces of description
Why climb a ladder and pray to colors

as if their names are impenetrable
vaults of latin snow

Why listen to witnesses
who have swiped quartz vertices

and their piped coughs
Why go toward the stages of sky

glowing through their amber bracelet
or sentence words to sentences

Why feed wingless instruments
gathering along bottom of last dream

to touch daylight's rim
Why leaving thinking for thought

Marden's Couplets

Was it inflections thinking themselves into dust
floating within the trajectories of their own ascent

Or was it just this thought thinking itself
back to where it began in and against

or thinking back to itself remembering
the lines becoming something other than,

more and less and maybe,
stone hard in their flayed insistence

that someone lived there once
breathed its airless dimensions

And then the eyes turning back to their task
picking up a line and following it down

toward and out over and through
thicknesses of light

trying to embrace something exhaling itself
toward the porous surface of its own held breath

For Brice Marden

Long slow path of dusky fluids
infiltrating daylight's weave

and the weave registering
the thickening and thinning

flow of each turn, the abrupt
and slow, at every instance

suspending an imprint,
a line, within the airy skin

Or I could say something in me
parts among the notes

within the bell
I will never see

as I step into the open,
onto the platform of this earth

in the above and below
of shadows and softening light

After Giorgio de Chirico

He saw them as two pears on a shelf
placed between us and him,
a woman's green breasts ripening
in the slow time of never drying earth

He stirred the fists of color
held inside his face,
their molded glints
still hardening in the parrot sky

The Invisible Painting Comes to Light

Independent crane operators stack earlier parades on the islands north of the capital. Others look for small pacified confines blooming with metal goods, wooden carriages, and fresh cocoa— places where trade has dwindled to small proportions, and tire strips, paraffin drippings, and cancelled stamps are among the most sought after items. Often, in the brightly bitten pandemonium of these cities, the women who clean the streets and water the flowerbeds wear clouds trimmed with antique words. Excess light collects in the muddy grottoes.

A maze of narrow alleys with morgues and chapels fills the interior of the factory. Anyone wishing to visit these stalls, their yellowing pages, must contact one of the many retired monks hanging around the animal necropolis on the outskirts of town.

When will the cinders fall from the sun, she asks the man examining her body. The pleasure of being two nightingales no longer brings sleep to our divided throats. The air is glass.

Piero di Cosimo's problem was that he was born too early in the wrong city. His fortune teller told him there was nothing to be done and smiled patiently, waiting for the coins to pierce the plane of color on which everything is foretold. Solution A. He would have to start listening to the dreams of those who could speak with someone else's tongue. Solution B. He would have to start remembering the dreams which showed him how to speak with his tongue.

The men gather in small groups and share the day's allotment of milk and cigars. One of them wears a dinosaur costume. Another stands his child up inside a wastepaper basket. Two flowers twisted into a bouquet. Accident reports and the remnants of games once played litter the floor on which no one is standing.

After Lew Welch's "After Anacreon"

I am the history you clock in front
the hook whose face you hang on

I wave lights at pink gobs
stop and watch you squeeze fire

from your oily lockets
I swipe widows of their little shine

I twist necks of rust to lease
more heat into swollen vents

I circle a ledge of gasps
and lisp back from the glare

while you stumble into
a spotted hair balloon

spilling lines of golden ooze

Three Sonnets:

Written Through Michael Gizzi's **Continental Harmony**

I count the sleeves
which are warm each time
I screw my eyes
to the twig of infinite pleasure
each time each vision
spans an arm of russet spittle
beside my voice I hear
the antlers fitting me to a tree
Tender is the missing head
its flagellant heart a memory
hooked up to blur the ocean
a wild gospel of weather
in which Coney Island lindens
are not native to sky's yellow scheme

Nutrition of the shelf outside the seam
Life of a torso without a spoon
Moonlight nippers fanned
Corrupt origin of the interred nose
Remnant of some iridescence
Lip hood picked off vest buzz
Cotton fume parlor prank

144

like that zipper mind
I am speaking to
hoists spatula sounds
hidden from their echoes
kisses their rumors
momentum of acoustic glimpses
wagging the palm of my shoe

Untouched miles stream through
the book of windy days
roll up cranium bars glacial finger
its decks of crystal attention
I got ducks and gadgets
to drift with a tongue
that makes the air grow
South of heaven the light switch's
fatal retread is missing the brush
its last strokes of reflection
leaping to the mind choir
I wear like my health explosive
attention brace shedding the fade
hair formation winding the music heave

Mulholland Voice Scatter

The bottom atmosphere had been cut into six equal precincts and spray painted red and gold. Beneath the slumber platforms, piles of black and yellow stones (or in local parlance the bumble fortune hats) were realigned, and a new set of illusion repeats were piped into the main display function.

A spotted hand pauses above the next sequence of buttons. It is late summer, a fresh brand of smog has started settling into the grooves above the bowling alleys along Paradise Mall. Time for the wind to make its glistening entrance.

The portable bubble of sweet blue air, a rumpled gray suit, and three day old breath laced with skirmishes and sour grape. The dreaded interruption. I was going to have drag my offensive lump out to the other end of town and identify the body. Someone with a dented gray fedora, greased down lips, and itchy left remnant was going to rename the parts.

Do you always keep an extra pair of nylons
locked inside in his mouth
Why do you make her watch the cramming
in a mirror

Can you track down the echoes
circling inside his hooded cries

She sighed inside a crowd of arm chair dust,
its tell-tale designs told her that a corpse
had listened to her radio while she was out
squeezing fresh staples.

Three umbrellas were haggling above the commotion.
People had difficulty deciding what clothes to wear
after the weather shifted from one broadcast era to
another.

It was the twentieth hour of the second thursday of the
thirteenth month. The day after collection day.

Album

A pockmarked child scrawls the last of the world's letters onto the rusting walls of an abandoned memory station. Another slightly less pockmarked child pins a wriggling shadow sliver to the wing of an extinct insect. So far, the narrative could begin: One writes down the shapes of yellowing sounds, while the other collects specimens whose names have slipped through the steel utility net.

Version B contains this insert: Two animals lick themselves and the jars forbidden to their offspring.

Version C starts: He made a camera out of a skull he found in the desert, on his car, or in the air (it was floating toward him).

Say this album is about the installment plan, the blackened chain of chapters, and the final payoff.

Say silver nitrate and milky white and the colors in between.

Say man with a dog's head or dog with a man's head.

Say a puddle of blood glistens in the courtyard.

Another possibility is that this is a coded message where one word stands for another. A gouged face, a yellow alarm clock.

The ancient story machine begins carefully copying down the shifts, bumps and variations. Crimson generator warranty airlift. The spotted hand and shriveled head of last century's most popular author are started up again. Shadows leave their shadows on a glass wall. The smallest bag of bumptious daydreams is numbered and filed.

Version D: A memory machine or box of memories, a turtle or a tureen.

Version E: Hermaphroditus steps from the seashell once reserved for Venus.

A flag of ashes lifts its waves above this city of alleyways, baskets, and pharmaceuticals. A red plasticene dove plunges into a blue tub, another sign that night is moving its cameras closer to our electric campfires. Meanwhile, the next watchdog allotment has zipped up their camouflage parkas and started their patrol. The winners of the afternoon's skirmishes are listed on the fence surrounding the flashlight factory.

One is Egyptian Water Coffin
Two is Visible Penetration.
Three is Rigid Ralph.
Four is Caterpillar Empress
Five is Six and Seven minus Eight.

Aztec priests divert the blood into a porcelain jar from China. The suction cups are cool and hard to the touch. Every day more ink splashes onto the corrupted formulas for fluid exchange.

149

I have turned the camera toward the chamber of overdoses. Serpent Suzy, Lucky Bingo, and the Twin Sobs.

A bridge of infected fur. The body is a labyrinth of gutters and streams, small moths flitting against the dirty retinas.

VIII

ANGEL ATRAPADO

Angel Atrapado I

We did not know we could fall safely from there to here, from
the sky's burgundy balcony, where we had been watching
ourselves sleeping, to the cracked and tilted slabs on which
we were walking. The name bolted to the side of the dented red
car means either "star" or "it does not go."

We did not know we could move among the city's inhabitants
as if they were letters of words spelling themselves out, shifting
particles and planes, beneath cloud filled skies. The downstairs
neighbor came up and announced "You must not throw ashes
in my face when you go out at night and look for the moon."

The birds do not leave the city except when they rise and circle
above its poured concrete towers, riding the currents twisting
and untwisting above the heat. The roses are almost the same
color as the zinnias in the painting above it, on the sunlit white
wall facing the mountain. A little man with three identical
heads stacked on top of each other. Books behind narrow
wooden door. Across the street, a dog barks at the shadow
inhabiting his favorite chair.

"This is the house of the Egyptian twins." Mountains,
benches, flowers. The preferred style for monuments is French,

a language found mostly in high priced restaurants near the museum. Brick ceiling above glass. Costumed waiters come with each marriage certificate.

It began "They wanted a woman who could collar drunks with duller cranks." It ended "We cooked some rumors, and began fanning the smoke across the river."

The blue panels of Edificio Sucre against the sky, one orange letter rising above the roof. Thick black lines float between definitions, either a crooked row of cardinal numbers or caricatures from the Encyclopedia of Outdated Emotions.

The red and gold Persian carpet from California.

You talked yourself into any knot but the one that let you breathe. You orbited the earth, a yellow angel.

He returns to the village of arson at dawn, his eyes on fire.

Angel Atrapado II

You were wearing my robe this morning, bottle green morning, yellow blossom robe, and I was standing there watching you advance toward me. This music holds us inside its shifting walls of spare winter notes. The man in the robe has your face, one of them, one of the ones you do not like, the others beings wings of blue smoke floating above the floors of an empty warehouse. Yes, the woman in the robe has your body, your flaccid bag of water and air. And she is waving it over her head, waving it like a flag.

I learned a lot from watching you masturbate, your legs crossed, your face contorted as if someone was sending electricity directly into your tongue.

He saw her in his mind's eye. Relaxed inside herself and the air she inhabited. Roaming alone inside that place inside herself. Smiling, eyes closed, head turned towards sky on other side of white wall. Shape of ankles, bones protruding, elegant fragile strong. Skin's tightness, hair's coarseness. It was all there inside him now, the place he roamed inside of, and toward.

I don't want to live inside my head, I want to live out of my body, live out of what my body wants. I want to know what it wants, listen to its impulses of hunger rising toward the surface.

155

I lived on the outside shelf, a jar facing the world of the handlers and the handled. I was a handle, something to grasp and lift and wash away. I don't want to live there anymore, but here in the flannel soot I am breathing.

In and among and in. Inside of but outside. Outside out there, and inside in here. How then to meet, make mesh and emerge.

We divided the remaining pronouns into two groups, the impersonal and the unlikely. Then we burned the dead, ground their bones into dust, and floated both them and their ashes down toward the main sewer plant. It was nearly spring. The buses were running again, and the air was filled with all different kinds of bookkeeping.

Every because is a catapult waiting for a snowflake to drop. The night is ferment and departure. My fingers are trembling as they unbutton the broken windows between us.

I was a monicker machine working the alley between the "you" and "I" we constructed in the garage. The wavering air was a blue coal. We watched it glowing in the fires we kept in our mouths.

Angel Atrapado III

We did not know how to dance when we met. We still
don't. And all the lingering has been dry, all our notions a
form of standing still and talking about what decorations we
need for the room we burn our faces in. I sent you a dance
mat and a prayer mat, each woven from the fiery hair of
children who pretended to be angels. Yes, and I sent you
green and violet parrots, keeping only one of their feathers
for myself.

I don't want you to look at what I'm doing. I want you to
watch but I don't want you to look. I want you to see
someone else doing this, someone you might want to get to
know if you had the chance.

It was winter—the sky was as white as a peach. We were
sitting on the porch of clouds floating above our wooden
lungs. A voice, neither yours nor mine, was heard between
where we were sitting and where we were dying.

I tried to tell him where to begin, but he would not listen. I
tried to tell him he had to follow the sequence or the order
would be wrong. I tried to tell him this was how the
sentences we were in would be written.

You must remember my daughter likes what I like. She likes to be pushed around. Only she has not had enough practice, at least not lately. I have. I have had a lot of practice, and you may want to try practicing on me before you go downstairs and see what song she is up to.

I made my way from the compound to the schoolyard. You were lying on the ground, waiting. We were supposed to undress and lie down next to each, embrace, but I don't remember how I knew this. All the children were blindfolded, some were singing and others clapping. A few tried to light their cigarettes. I couldn't speak, I couldn't tell you what I wanted you to do. You understood this, got up, and covered your eyes when we kissed.

Angel Atrapado IV

It was my body I was watching. I was both in it and constructing it, both in the pool of the pleasure it was receiving and quietly building low sinuous walls to prevent its liquids from flowing away. I was a man or a woman or both. I was looking at it, walking toward it, was lying there waiting to be reached.

The scene was a movie or sentences resembling a movie, isolated instances melting into each other when they were not. I was the camera or arrow (the eyes that see the scene but the body that is not in it) moving across the screen in front of me, making the details of what was taking place there assume a life of their own. And in their own life, these sentences became bodies moving about before me. I saw them, was them, but did not know whether the "I" that I was seeing was mine or not.

The scene changed or became clearer, I couldn't decide. I saw this mute "I," it was a he. He was lying there. Another he (perhaps another me) was approaching. It was a surgeon, someone who could perform operations, could dissect a body into its different sentences, its separate lines of information. I couldn't tell if he was giving information to the one lying on the table or taking it away. I couldn't tell what I was being given to read.

159

It was the only way I could be there seeing this scene, as a picture looking down at a table, the body or book that used to be mine. Someone, perhaps you, gave it to me, and then took it away, giving me a book describing a body, giving me the outline of what I used to inhabit. I was what was missing from its pages, I was what was not being written there, a place emptied of all voices. The "I" that you crushed when it first cried out, the one trying now to speak to the body or book it once inhabited. The "I" was what was removed, the "I" now looking back at what is there.

Angel Atrapado V

The words he is writing down are starting to interfere with the ones he whispers in his sleep. He saw himself write these words down, and wondered what they were going to say back to him. Busy dreams above busy murmurs, he was alone in his room, standing on his desk, listening to the one inside him whispering to the one sitting beneath the lamp, the one who learned how to pretend he was visible, and the one who lied whenever he spoke.

We were wearing tin wings painted silver, and standing on either side of the broken bed. To be an angel is to shed the body, to float above the clouds gathering inside the names you use when you leave the room. To be an angel is to announce the things to come, sentences passing through altars of water, emptying into the alleys between us, between us and the sky, between the sky we cannot reach and the earth we never visited.

I was watching you look for the names that had been written inside your mouth, the ones you couldn't spit out.

We were together without knowing how each of us fit into the space reserved for us, the space formed out of the space between declarations and lies, the stories we wove around our

bodies even as we pushed them across the table, our bodies
on the table, writhing beneath a bright yellow light.

Even as it says over and over this is the voice you keep saying
is yours, you keep trying to say what it is you want to say.
All the many voices singing at once. All the many inside you
rising toward the surface of the voice you sleep inside of.
O curled rodent, broken cane, old and worn towel stolen
from a desert star. O the things you try not to become when
their shadows move themselves toward you.

I was wearing a blue shirt, and I was climbing the stairs to
meet you. I was ringing the wrong bell, and I was
introducing myself to someone who believed in errors. It was
part of the plan, the other reproduction already delivered to
the wrong factory by mistake.

I was in the attic, leaning over a doll lying in a red dump
truck, a doll with skin like yours, except that it had gotten
old and didn't glisten in the moonlight the way you did
when I splashed your skin with tears, and bit your face until
it glowed like an apple.

Search me, mark me, and then deliver the remaining contents
of my image to the window where you are standing, speaking
to the voices roaming the air behind you.

Angel Atrapado VI

This fruit will change color in one day, lose its fragrance in two. I am sending it to you under a laurel green parasol, along with the tongues of all those I heard praise your beauty behind your back. Now, even if you never again leave the halls of your white marble dormitory, the perfumes of what they would have said next will float around you.

I hid my first language inside my second, spoke to you in a voice I had sifted from the pages lodged between them, their dials of dawn spinning in my hands.

We were driving a car named after a city of gold, a city that was invented by the people living in these mountains so that all travelers would want to keep going. I was a squalid dog, listening to stammers punctuating a container of signals, its blue enamel breath. You were still turning inside the dream's cassock. On your lap a lidded box, and resting inside it were the stones known as "a horse's brain." What was I to do? I got down on my knees and drank the doll's water.

We were standing on the unadorned terrace, counting the clouds extinguishing the mountain. You told me that I was an asteroid or an ostrich, that I was vapor rising from rotting bones, that I had been with you before I met you, and that we had bruised ourselves pressing against the air between us. It was in another city, one where pain was not necessarily something the body felt or the mind remembered.

We were inside each other once more, looking for mirrors without a past.

We couldn't decide if the sky was an omnivorous antenna or a receiving junction.

I forced myself to speak to you, the words rising from my mouth after I set myself on fire, the smoke drifting toward you or towards where you had just been, outline of crumpled grass, and the sky clinging to your ankles as you walked toward the river.

Yes, I was listening to the rain, but hovering above and below wet perimeters, still pearls, and the creviced dark.

I wanted to tell you about the dreams I copied down in the days before I swam toward the surface, its zone of light and nutrients. I wanted to show you the pebbles balanced on the tip of my yellow tongue, the stories clustered around them like flies.

164

Angel Atrapado VII

The one who says: I was almost alive or nearly dead or
somewhere in between, a dirty flask full of second hand tears.
I thought I was inside this room inside myself, but I was
walking past the window. I saw you listening to what was being
said, examining the syllables, their cold sibilants, and then
holding them up and asking what they were that you too could
use them. But we hadn't yet spoken, nor (as it turned out)
would we ever.

The one who says: They want to be friends but they cannot
help themselves, and think it is business. Or they think they are
moving towards business when they want to be friends. The
one who licks his or her golden lips when you expose your
neck, raise your head above the words you have been trained to
follow all along.

The one who says: I grow inside you growing inside me, feel
your voice inside the voice used to speak, the voice falling back
into itself, the voice barely able to listen to itself listening, the
voice full of borrowed words sent forth in borrowed clothes,
the voice of that one over there lying under the bed, asking for
something other than money but metallic nevertheless.

The one who says: An imbecile and his rabbit huddle under a decrepit family tree. A coolie and a taxi dancer run past the underworld. A robot and its patient argue over chess.

Or is it the one who says: I am watching bullet riddled bodies tumble beneath the final layers of evening's gift, their pastel colors describing a wall beyond the horizon, and what is taking place in front of me has started burning through all the pages held up to the light.

Or is it finally the voice cursing itself for having spoken at all, that one and that one and that one, and all of them pushing toward the mouth or empty sky they once thought was theirs and theirs alone.

Angel Atrapado VIII

Where will this voice go once it leaves me, leaves the mouth kissing pockets of air as if one of us has left the room? Someone said these words, someone running behind the one who is silent, the one elected to speak by the ones whose language does not fit their tongues. Someone said: It will dissolve in the shadows pressing themselves against us, it will run down the walls of sunlight filling the room you lease when you are in the company of others. Someone said these words, someone floating face down in a bathtub full of food.

I wanted to see you swimming between the pages of a book, all the words in profile. I wanted to hear you talk about the oracular menaces infiltrating the daily rust.

It was the hour of the day when the flames thicken, and smoke climbs its ladders and blocks out the sun. You told me you wanted to see if I could find you, who was burning one of your faces off beside the library of stolen books.

You were paid to throw oranges at a man old enough to be your uncle. Not your father's age, but your uncle's, this was the distinction. An uncle was someone you threw oranges at, someone who smiled at the juice running down his chest.

I tried stealing what was mine, you whispered. I tried stealing the body I once slept in and wore, the one that looks like something is missing from the air it breathes, the one I had been using as a ramp.

This time it will be different, you tell yourself. This time you won't swallow the nails you carry inside your mouth. This time you won't impale your tongue on a knitting needle, offer it to those whose tails have been severed from the rugs heaped in front of the fireplace.

This honey will inhibit thirst.

This word was used to fill the space between one thing and another.

This shadow was once attached to its base.

This photograph will make it impossible for you to remember me.

Escape, he was told, was unacceptable. You cannot escape from your life into mine. You must do something else. You must reach me without leaving, must reach me who is looking through the place where you are standing. Yes, I am inside the mirror, and I am watching you.

Angel Atrapado IX

How do you say goodbye to the cold one out there or the invisible one in here, the one who cannot speak or the one whose voices sometimes overtake yours? Who was it who was just speaking, he thought. Whose accusation was whispering beneath his tongue? The one lying still or the one he never sees, the one whose shadows he has felt falling across him when he was looking at someone speaking, the words floating between them. Or the one who is almost quiet while he is walking to and from the window he hides behind, the window of speech, the window he can neither open nor close.

I had fallen back to earth, but I had not fallen back into my body. When I woke up I was looking at the sky hovering above the trees, and someone with whiskers was kissing the blisters boiling in my brain.

He told me I should get a couple of cases of whisky and call in the potential heating men of the city and give them anything they wanted—a floor show and all the liquor they could drink. He called it my first lesson. He told me that in my second lesson I would learn what to do about the altar, what to do when anyone came near it or me.

I was the rubble and the riddle, a string of crooked premonitions and a delicate fragrance trapped in city heat. I was hired to slice and mount thin sections of dead tissue, while others argued over how to compensate the man in the flowered shirt who announced: I am a civilized servant working in an uncivilized environment. I am an advertisement for a brain too stupid to understand other brains. At noon, I pointed to the slide and grinned: it looks like we are going to have to resort to metaphors. It looks like we are going to have to realize that despite the impression given by the speaker, no one has actually seen any of this happen.

I lay back on the leather banquette and trembled. I lifted the shaving brush to my lips, turned toward the window, and looked for evidence of your face or mine. Why have you commanded me to rest? Why should I confess that I want shouts and claps at every pause? Why do I want to spin my body like a giddy wheel or dance among the vulgar throng of voices rising within my speechless lies?

I am a flap of blue flannel, something soaked in grease, and my tongue is stuck between my mouth and the air it cannot reach.

Can you say when you began hearing the voices swirling inside you, speaking as if you weren't there? Can you say when you began hearing yourself talk to the one who isn't there, the one beside you? It was the day I knew that whatever I had was going to change me into itself, a table of elements smeared on glass, a cross section of dirty water. It was the day I felt an alien music switch the channels intersecting my body.

170

Angel Atrapado X

All those gathered in the assembly began standing up and speaking. In my last life, I was the son of a merchant who beat me across the back with a pair of glowing tongs. Before that I was the daughter of a jealous rival, one of a long line of smilers banished to blackened chapters, and condemned to sweat beneath vinyl canopies. Recently, I tried to prevent further interference, momentum, and shifts, but a fly began circling inside my voice.

We will be the transportation, the bicycle or bobsled, the hill or gravel path. Then we will drink our flasks of human acid, and drift out past the hinges of falling stone, the platforms crowded with martyrs trying to call home.

It is only now that I realize I was confusing the bell with the voice answering the bell, the voice hampered by the docile propellor peeling back the sun. You were there, or someone like you, someone so like you that you had become the one I was addressing. I was there, in the noise of the ashes and lamplight. Yes, I was there, in the middle of the sentence, its balcony of vibrations, and there was nothing else I could do but jump into the linoleum, plastic, and wood.

He liked to unbutton my blouse in front of his mother. That's one reason, the other is not worth mentioning, at least not here, not now, not while we are where are, doing what we are doing. No, in this air, its red velvet box, I would like us to stay as we are—two parrots nodding and screeching, broadcasting snippets of tales told to us by one legged men in their foolish old age.

How can I be worried about her? She is up there. She is beautiful. And she has a brain. A man's brain.

Certain phrases or starts of the body begin to be inter-changeable at every juncture, corners where words meet words.

She was talking again, the motor humming in the dream's backyard, the air full of its own decaying light. I was skimming through my wardrobe, checking the moisture levels and bacterial growth. This is perfume from the Milky Way, you said. This is sap we twisted from our bones.

Angel Atrapado XI

I eat rice with two wooden sticks.
I beat lice with burning wicks.

The one without clothes is speaking to the one without a tongue. Who
were they, he thought, and why were they the ones he was
seeing and hearing when he closed his eyes. The window is
open, and the sky is floating between where he is standing and
what he is looking at, what cannot be seen though it is there,
in what is called the "outside" though it is not where it is
supposed to be, but is a span of thought suspended among
words. This is what it is like to hear someone speaking to the
name he is called by others. This is where he thinks he is when
their words reach him, where he is standing or sitting and
listening.

Once I wore my father's suit. Another time, while they were
out having dinner with friends, I put on my mother's dress,
traipsed out the front door, hailed a cab on the corner, rode
past the soft bright rooms and down the dusty flanks. It didn't
matter. I was still there, still inside what I didn't want to be
inside of, flagrant flesh and its musty cling.

I didn't want to be in the window of what you were saying, all the words piling up, sweet mounds of flowers, perfume of what you said infiltrating the air's provinces.

The plane has more wings than people holding it above the wind. I was one of the struts, one of the columns lifting it above the villagers, their swaying rage finally bursting through the last veil of decorum they carried with them whenever they rode into the next village.

You hide the words behind you. Then you hide behind the words, using them to deflect all inquiry, as if you could keep moving forever, as if that moving isn't also a way of speaking. You tell me that each time you open your mouth and talk, you are telling me something more about who you actually might be, you are interrupting yourself.

Angel Atrapado XII

The one who says: You were not talking, but you were listening to yourself talk. Remember, the first blow will stun you, and the second will bring you to your senses. You must find a seat directly in front of the platform, where their increasingly vigilant eyes cannot find you.

The one who says: It was you who was sitting in the chair just now, it was you who was speaking to the voices inside you, remembering the past of a minute ago, its illuminated pages glowing behind your eyes.

The one who says: Words intelligible to one side of the brain remain incoherent to the other. It is called "speaking in one's own tongue," the voice that emerges when you talk in your sleep. You might one day hear the edge of it fading, your eyes opening on a bus, or beside someone who looks like you, a brother or sister if you had one.

The one who says: You must learn to read the inscriptions on your forehead, the letters carved in bark, all that is grandiose and tasteless, all that has been left to you by those who gave you your name, the one you did not register under, the one you let rot in your mouth as you sat in the hotel lobby, waiting for a cab.

The one who says: I lived around the clock from her.

The one who says: You are not escaping, but you are leaving. The one who tried to escape must return. Now that you have started changing the middle tenses you must live in their corridors, large open rooms to the side of the muzzle you once made out of the clouds, the coats of warm dust they brought with them.

The one who says: Her black skirt rises up when she stands and walks towards the door, sunlight illuminating the triangle formed by her legs and the floor, the skirt a diaphanous veil. The one who imagines what he wants and the one who wants what he imagines, their stories erasing themselves and each other in the window of their telling.

The one who says: I feel a convulsion, a melting within.

The one who says: The food you call garbage is too sweet and too delicious to gather with just one hand.

Or perhaps it is the one who says: The house of crocodiles is near a shapeless mass of mud and brick. Green water oozes from the eyes of a saint. The skeletal arm of a woman lies among the stones piled below your window. She is waiting to be gathered up and placed behind glass.

Or is it the one who points to the one who is unable to listen? Or the one who listens but cannot speak? Or the one who says: You must buzz the snitches hiding behind the owl's smile. You must find the exit from Slice Town.

Angel Atrapado XIII

I am looking for the one who says: stick your tongue out at the mirror and see the eyes engraved in the soft copper parts of your acid flesh.

I am looking for the one who says: you must speak to the one out there who is listening, the one in the tall chair who has tiny feet and tinier hands, the one who speaks back in words that reach your doorstep, that slide in through the cracks, that settle like dust on the table where you are tracing your name in the snow, over and over.

I am looking for the one who says: you must use these words, these or any words, as if they were yours or someone else's, as if they will spell the outline of your body into the pink and green air surrounding the fist you carry inside the brain you have mounted on your head, the one whose face is hidden from itself and others.

I am looking for the one who says: there is nothing to finish saying but you must begin using them up nevertheless, the words disguised as mist, the words behind the words, the words placed on the tip of your tongue like molten gold, the ones you have been trying to spit out ever since you first gasped for air.

177

I am looking for the one who says: I will hear you on the undivided stairs of speech rising from your mouth. I will gather the sand you requested, the pockets of wind, buckets of air, and trinkets of rain, all that is needed to assure you the day has already arrived, bringing with it the gray remains of colors once used to describe a face.

I am looking for the one who says: the dimensions and weight of your brain are listed on the obverse side of the ankle bracelet you carry beneath your tongue, in the mouth that neither opens nor closes, the one inside the one you have never used, the one speaking to you now.

I am looking for the one who says: this face, its yellow headlights, is the one you will wear when I am speaking through you to the one out there you think is you.

Angel Atrapado XIV

It could have been, it was, and maybe now it will be once more. It could have been, but it wasn't, and now I am here, waiting to be there. It could have been, I tell you this over and over because I am still there, a penetrated shadow, waiting for you to circle by, take me to wherever you went, however and why ever you did it left by me on a desk of dust and rain, place where someone traced the inlets of my thighs, place where I became a pen outlining my body, soft thing you obtained through the intimacy of mail.

I am looking at the one without clothes standing behind a name I recognize and talking in a language I understand but do not speak.

You asked, how do you shuttle from that world, its shelf, to this one, from out there, beside the grove of blue and yellow stalks, to in here, the red and green rug of silk and money?

You asked, how do I know you hear me unless you do what I say, follow the plan I have for you, the one I want you to grope for in my wet warm dark.

I am kneeling on the other side of the air we were supposed to inhabit, the one that would carry us past the end of this story, the one that would tell us another story has started to occur, the one that would dissolve the rooms inside the story we placed between ourselves and each other.

You whispered, someone stands between each of our pronouns so that when one of us is speaking, he or she doesn't know which of them has taken control.

You whispered, someone throws a head, someone swings a bat. Midnight's coal tumbles toward the fire.

You whispered, someone wags an empty head, someone waves an empty tongue.

Angel Atrapado XV

Someone likes you, someone like you. Or is it? *Someone like you, someone likes you.* In the castle of mirrors one of us turns to sand, while the other polishes the stones floating beneath his or her tongue.

We were talking about getting inside the place we were in, the one you described and the one I pointed to, a schoolhouse burning between them.

We were talking about the distance one needs to see the other clearly through the lens of pronouns and verbs, the little mudcaked skull of illumination we, one of us, carry, while the other gets down on his or her knees and tries to decipher the words appearing on the screen.

All the air is mine as this body, my body, is yours to twist off its locks. Drink from it and be thirsty. All this snow is mine, wash in it, and I will come and greet you with my tongue of bright glass, dry the bones you are hiding beneath your skin.

I wear clothes that resemble a box, something stamped and written on, something moved from place to place, something torn open.

I stalk two rangers.
I talk to strangers.

Is not in knots. About and beside. Or maybe now and not
again. Or maybe again but not now. Yes, some songs sing
themselves through the mouth of the one who doesn't speak,
hand pointing to the water of the air inside, strings tightened
to the point of sweet excess.

Or maybe the words we bring to the air outside our mouths
leads us away from here, toward rooms and clouds that have
yet to open.

Angel Atrapado XVI

The one who says: You will rise to the surface of an old
dream, its small varnished bubble, and enter another dream,
where a radio of air is waiting to fill your mouth with sand.
Or was it the one who says: You will dwindle away, leaving
this room and your blanket for another congregation of
particles.

I was watching you dance before the mirror, drying your hair
and arching your back. I was listening to you point the
words toward me, their arrowheads dipped in the motions of
your mouth. I began hearing you whisper: My tongue is a
turtle, its head locked inside the words I place around my
name. I am the seasons inside my body, windy days
proceeding towards the northern dust. I was born during
either the Feast of Chickens or the Festival of Dragon Dung.
I was born after I burned the wires lacing my head.

We are each other's fireplace, something to stand in front of
and get warm, something to take us away from where we are
singing.

I was the smallest member of the penguin chorus.
I was the youngest hero of the iceberg wards.

The car veered towards the gap between them, its headlights focused on the wall they had previously been facing, watching the shadows blackened by others.

She read him a story about a rabbit beheaded by a grandmother, a doll locked in a closet full of dirty ties. He was told it was not a warning but an indication, a word he would have to look up later, after all the stars had been glued in place.

The parade of camels and bears began passing before the jolly mayor and his three ex-wives. The outcasts had been laughed at in a manner becoming to both them and their tormentors. Knowing no one would see us leave, we climbed inside one of the few empty bathtubs and started confessing what each of us suspected the other had held back. You said we were beginning to tell a story that had not quite started. We were beginning to learn if the right words could tempt us away from our bodies, the fan-shaped ones we had previously offered to strangers with sharp gleans and broken stands.

Angel Atrapado XVII

There was nothing left to send you, so I fashioned this from
smoke and hair, from the remains of the day as they were
handed to me by others, by those who lost their tongues and
those who forgot how to speak. It was the beginning of
winter or the end of fall, it was dawn or dusk, it was yes
I am here, and no I am not.

Your words—are they yours or are they what I heard after
you stopped speaking?—continue to ring inside the well, the
column of cold air we sank into the earth.

You are neither as big as you claim to be, nor as small as I
said you are. I was remembering the size of your words when
you said this, when you repeated them in a soft voice, the
one you used to use just before you turned on the yellow
light. You were standing with your back to me, talking about
the buttons you would need to fix the shirt or blouse, the
color of his hair when he was a puppy, the way water tasted
after you came out of the jungle, down from the mountains.
The radio is playing our song, you said, the one that brought
us here.

Inside of, then outside. Always these two places, no window
or wall between them. You could get to think, you could

begin, somewhere you do, but not here, not in this place you are inside of, the outside here too.

Pees or please, sees or flees. You as the object, the one whose mouth tries to empty itself of the words leading to your shadow.

We were talking about international terrorism, about the voices one hears in airports, about the weather and how it affects our choice of colors, about why it is necessary to let some people starve and others grow fat.

Or is it just the one who says: blaze and pant. Or the one who whispers: they have human feet and wear helmets shaped like stars, like units of sound locked inside a music box. Or is it the one who points to the pieces of rope dangling from our waists, their lengths determined by the weight of greed each of us carries beneath our tongues. Or is it the one who writes: He must have mounted a camera in his mouth, he must have known I had fished him in the car.

Angel Atrapado XVIII

I wake up dreaming that I am in a room telling you about
the dream I just had in which we were crowded beneath a
ledge waiting for that portion of ourselves that leaves each
night to return from the cave where someone maybe you or I
is waiting to speak. I have risen from sleep into a dream I tell
myself but you say no this is not what is passing beneath us,
like water. It is a reflection you are looking at and I am the
one standing behind you, undressing, motioning you to turn
around and see the wet purple sky I am offering, the bruise
you left on my dry yellow tongue.

Something besides a fish flopping on the table.
Something besides a fist dropping through the air.
Something else crawls inside the dish.
Something resembling a broken disk.

I didn't want you to reach the end of the sentence I was
writing, the one I am revising, the one you should return to,
become part of, all the nouns and verbs of my body at your
disposal.

Please becomes a new lease on strife. The please piece left
outside the wooden door to your art. I was stalking again. I
was one of the shadows sent into the city.

Plump
lump
ump

He heard the letters fall away and wrote down the remains.
A string of molecules dissolving in the ether. They were the
names of someone he knew, himself or another, hidden
behind the syllables.

The one who says: I wish I had known you in another life,
in another passage of time. The one who holds that now in
front of you, as if either of you could get there. The one
who says: It is there. All you have to do is find your way.
The one who says: I am sorry that you have to start over.
And the one who never speaks is still looking at you,
wondering what there is to see. Or so the other one says, the
one who knows what everyone is thinking.

IX

FIVE PIECES

The Story of Our Life

Last time
the first
in many
years

She was
to have
her heart
checked

stopped before
getting in car
was like a child
so often in her life

was this time
reluctant to go
was scared
and stubborn

afraid
to admit
her fear
lose face

except this once
when she could not
hold
back

(her strength
or was it
her stubbornness
gone)

and turned
and held me
kissed me
and would not let go

so that
at one time
or another
one of us

was pushing
against
or prying
the other away

A Story for Your Story

In her letter was a story, and in her story was a letter. In the letter containing the story, she told me she had been thinking of him while she was swimming. The story of a movie she had seen when she was a child, a western. In the movie a woman is rescued from the Indians by a cowboy, who lifts her off the ground onto the horse he is riding. She remembers reenacting this scene with her older sister, who could never manage to lift her swiftly and gracefully off the ground. They practiced it over and over, trying to achieve the impossible.

The story included precise descriptions of two memories, and, by being juxtaposed with one another, they suggested the links that might exist between their occurrence and a desire she no longer had, to be lifted from the ground as if her body was a letter.

The story was about two people who had met and decided to continue without knowing what would happen next. The story was about the woman telling the story and the man who would read it later on. She will tell him the story when she puts it in a letter she sends to him, a letter he reads shortly after sending her one in which he tells her that he is having trouble thinking of her because things have started lodging themselves between himself and his thoughts, and that these other thoughts, their things, are difficult to lift and put aside. He has to write them down. And the act of writing them down, of rendering into written words the noise he hears inside his head, the articulation of black profiles on a white field, makes them smaller. He sends her the words that have made it difficult for him to send the words telling her that he is thinking about her. He tells her that only by writing down what he is hearing in his head can he understand what some of the voices are saying, voices that breathe inside him but are not his own. It is how he gets from here to here.

The man reading the story has not seen the western she is remembering. In the movie he remembers seeing as a child, at about the same age she was when she saw the western, there were two characters, a young boy and his father, who was a truck driver, an independent. Either the movie never explains the mother's absence or he couldn't remember. The father took the son with him whenever he made a long trip. One night the truck got a flat tire. The father pulled over by the side of a dark, deserted road, and tried to put a new tire on. The jack slips and the father is pinned under the truck. The scene he remembers is always the same: the camera is tightly focused on the faces of the helpless father and the terrified son.

194

The camera is a fountain drinking this scene in, a wall of grissaille light. All the surfaces glisten, like the tears falling down the young boy's cheeks. Everything—the black tar road, the background of fluttering leaves, the truck's dented metal—seems wet, and ready to cry. It is as if the film itself has just emerged from a thick, clear puddle.

The man remembers the scene vividly, but cannot remember what happens next. The movie, his memory of it, stops at the scene of the accident. The camera is focused on the crying boy and the reassuring father. For him, a father reassuring his son was something that happened only in the movies.

In her story she describes a letter a father wrote his son. The letter is about the mother, who is dead, and what she said about her son, the man reading the story, before she died. It was a story the father had made up.

☆

In her story she does not write about happened next. The son tries to move away from the circle of words the father encloses in his letter. The son decides that instead of talking to his father on the phone, he will answer him in a letter.

He wants the time it takes for a letter to travel from one city to another to be his way of marking the space between them. He wants to make the spaces between his father's words wide enough for him to emerge unscathed. He wants to achieve the impossible; he wants to have his father hear him.

☆

He writes the letter in simple declarative sentences, numbering the memories, all of them sitting like boulders or fallen trees in the road between his house and his father's.

☆

The father reads the letter, and, instead of calling, responds with his own list. An accountant, he details the exact sums of money he believes his son still owes him. He mails the letter, knowing that he will soon be dead of cancer. He wants the boulders and fallen trees to be permanent. He wants to make sure that nothing can move them, and that if by some miracle they are moved, the house at the end of the road will be empty.

☆

He learns that he owes money for a dinner they had twenty years ago, learns the amount of a long distance phone call he made from their home. Everything is accounted for down to the penny.

☆

196

In her story, there are two memories, one of a movie she saw when she was a child, and the other of an accident that occurred while a movie was being made near where she lived after she graduated college. The accident was the result of the director's belief in perfection, that reality was something that could be mimicked so perfectly that the audience would for a moment believe they were seeing the way certain historical events actually unfolded. It was about how memory could be reenacted, and time made to stand still long enough for what had happened to happen again, only this time, in the movie, without anyone dying. But the scene the actors had to keep practicing collapsed, and they fell from fiction into fact.

☆

The man reads the letter containing the story mentioning the letter. He has two memories, though he will discover later when he talks to her that only one of them might be true. He remembers reading her the letter he sent to his father, and the one he received a few weeks later. In the movie he saw when he was a child, the light of the story empties into the theater, the audience's eyes drinking it all in. For him, the camera stops, and the scene is frozen. A young boy crying, a father reassuring him. He remembers the scene, but until he reads her story, and learns of her childhood desire to be lifted off the ground, and carried away, he has never been sure why he remembers it.

☆

In his memory, the camera never moves beyond a scene that occurs somewhere in the middle of the movie. As a young boy sitting alone in the theater, he continued watching the

197

movie, which probably had a happy ending. The woman saw
another movie, which presumably also had a happy ending.
He thought of happy endings as false interruptions, as ways
of pretending to move towards some truth, that the audience
wanted to believe that happy endings were a common
occurence, and that they could by identifying with someone
in the movie become part of its story, part of its happy
ending.

☆

They live in different cities in different countries. She sends
him a story she has written, and he begins writing one in
response. The scene he remembers has burned through the
movie until all that remains of the story is a fragment he sees
himself watching, a young boy sitting in shadows looking at a
young boy made of changing gray light.

☆

There are stories others tell in an attempt to enclose the
listener, and stories you tell trying to release yourself from
the words of others. Some stories are fragments of something
larger, something half forgotten, initially ignored, or
misremembered. She tells him a story about trying to move
out of their stories, their telling, into her own. She uses parts
of stories told by others.

☆

In the film he saw, an accident was made to look real, while
in the film she read about in the newspaper an accident

interrupted the rescue the actors were rehearsing. Both directors wanted their films to become large mirrors, rectangles of reflective light held up to the audience. In each movie, the audience saw someone they could identify with moving through a story they could imagine as being a metaphor or echo of their own. The newspaper told about the inevitable, that all stories are eventually interrupted, that they continue in different forms with different characters.

They had gone to the movies when they were children, had started seeing and remembering them long before they decided to meet each other one night and go to a movie.

At the movies, they sat in large dark rooms and saw stories that did not reflect them, reflected instead what they were not nor could ever be. A girl who is as light as a feather, a boy who can lift trucks.

He looked at what he had written. *She wrote a story and sent it to him. He read it, and began using what she said to say something back. In this way they were able to begin talking, two people who had reached a point where talking of any kind had become a far bigger act than it actually was. Memory's incompleteness, he thought, all its fragments are echoes of a story, a story that cannot be heard or quite told to another, a story you try to hear, its voices all speaking at once, that noise, both a mirror and an interruption.*

Photographs for an Album

I

One brother had trouble bonding, while the other practiced forms of bondage. This was something he discovered when he returned from their father's funeral with a roll of film, not copies of the photographs the funeral owner took of their father in his casket, gray blue skin and thin white hair carefully arranged so as to look natural. He had not asked his brother for those, had not asked them to be taken though they were because his brother had asked for them, as their father had when his wife, their mother, had died and was lying in her casket in the same funeral home six months earlier.

The photographs showed him something he had suspected for a long time, but now that he had the proof in his hands he did not know what he would say to the one with his back to the camera, the one in chains hoisted off the floor.

The one who had trouble bonding wanted to say something to the one who was chained. He remembers that he has been told that he has had trouble speaking, and it was this trouble, this stone in his mouth, that eventually kept him from speaking to those who were supposed to be close to him, his parents and brother, his wife.

The one who had trouble bonding did not live with he had once lived with, having chosen to live by himself in a full of books. The one who practiced bondage continued in the house of their parents, the house full of accusing and faces that never registered what was being said to the house they would leave to their two sons.

The one who was in bondage was never home, and

who found it difficult to speak found it difficult to keep calling, not knowing what he would say about the roll of film he had had developed, the pictures of his brother, naked and in chains, a blonde woman in dark glasses holding a whip and smiling into the camera.

There was a moment when he thought this was where all humor came from, that laughter was an expression of the desire to keep moving, a way of releasing the voices he heard into the air around him.

After the funeral, he had picked up the camera he had seen sitting on the desk in the living room, and driven back to a town the family once lived in. He and a friend, someone he hadn't seen in many years, hadn't seen since the poison used to kill foliage, a poison named after a color, had infiltrated his body. They drove through the streets, down past names familiar and unfamiliar, toward the rooms he once lived in, and classes he once sat in.

He was in a dream, a story made of streets he both knew and didn't know, other voices now unfolding in the rooms he once sat in, with his eyes closed, dreaming.

His friend had taken the last pictures on the roll, including one of him standing on the steps of his high school. It was a cold spring day, the day he and his brother stood, watched, and listened to others speaking about their father. During the service, his brother turned to him and asked: Did he have any brothers and sisters? Or was he an only child?

He was an only child though he had never spoken about his childhood.

Each parent loved one son and hated the other. One would be beaten, and the other would be ignored. The beatings would stop, but the neglect would not. When the one who had trouble bonding tried to speak to the parents about this, they would look at him as if he were speaking about another family, about people they had never met and didn't know. To them it was nothing more than a story.

II

He remembers the album his parents kept in a bookcase in the living room, a few years before his brother was born. In one section there were many photographs of his mother and her family, and in the other section were the captions, all written in white ink on black paper, that identified the photographs that had been removed, images of the war his parents had survived, events his father had recorded on film. He remembers lying on the floor and trying to see the pictures the words pointed to, trying to imagine what was no longer there. He remembers looking carefully at the grainy gray photographs in newspapers and wondering if they were similar to what his father had seen. He remembers his father pummeling him with a belt after he pointed a toy gun at him.

III

Before dying their father had started putting together an album. Piles of photographs on the table beside his bed, the dark downstairs room of the house he and his wife lived and died in. It was the story of their life, his and hers, and then later the two sons. It was this story, his arrangement of it, that the minister spoke of at the funeral. It was the story of two people sending love poems to each other, love poems written in a foreign language, the language which their children would learn first. It was a story he had never heard before, a story he almost believed because he knew that to his father it was a true story, a story of a man and woman who sailed to America, a story in which they had been separated from their families, and then from their country and language. It was a story of rooms inside rooms inside rooms. And now, thinking of the photographs of his brother, he wondered if another room had been erected inside him, a room with chains dangling from the ceiling, a room his brother secretly enters in search of consolation.

Photographs for an Album (Second Version)

I

One brother liked to watch a woman undress, while the other brother liked to wear women's dresses. There are some things you think you will never mention, but one day you begin talking about them, he thought. One day you begin talking about them knowing that is not what you want to be doing, but you go on talking, go on as if there is nothing else to talk about, as if you are talking about someone else, someone you made up.

Made up, he thought. Someone you make up, someone in make-up. He made himself up as he put on his make-up. It was not make believe, it was someone someone made up, someone you see looking back, looking back from that place in which you are encased, frozen face covered in something other than ice.

He was sitting in his apartment, looking at the photographs, knowing without wanting to know that the talking had already started, that the voices had already entered his thoughts, had already become part of what he would or would not say. Now they were inside him too, photographs of his brother hanging in chains, wearing a shiny black dress, kissing the shoes of a woman whose face was left out of view, long black whip dangling from her gloved hand.

II

The brother who liked to watch a woman undress had removed the photographs from an envelope, expecting to see something else. An image of himself standing on the steps of his high school,

203

twenty-five years after he graduated without honors of any sort, not the image of his brother hanging naked from the ceiling.

You cannot speak of the deprivation of someone else as if it is something that happened to you, something you own. You cannot speak of the events that marked you or your brother, the things that made you up, the make-believe rooms you entered in order to get away from the ones you were in. You cannot tell either his story or your own. So you sit there looking at the photographs of your brother hanging in chains and wonder what you can say to him or anyone else about what you are looking at. You wonder who would listen to this if you began. You wonder why. You wonder what you would say, why you would say it. You cannot speak for others, he thought. You cannot take their place.

III

The one hanging in chains and the one looking at him are brothers. One left their parents' house while in high school, the other moved back there after college. The one who left spoke to his parents about the one who was living with them and they laughed. Though he never admitted it, the one who stayed at home was angry at the one who left because one parent loved him and one parent hated him, and he was stranded between their choices. Or was it that the one who stayed at home was loved and hated in another way? he thought. Ways that he knew were in his imagination rather than his memory, because he had left home as soon as he could, leaving them—father, mother, and his brother—behind.

204

IV

Once he wrote a story about a brother waiting for his older brother to return, an older brother he imagines having, one who left before he was born, and whose abrupt departure caused his parents to become what they had become, two listless shadows staring into themselves, two mouths speaking about what it was like before he was born. In his story, the younger brother is sitting alone on the porch, watching the cars pass. It is late evening, near fall. The light has started to change.

After finishing the story he put it away and didn't read it again for many months. He told himself he had written a story, and he had wanted to write something else, something that would hold something else inside of it, something he had not been able to inject into what he had written. Was it that he wanted to tell a story that held something inside of it? something that he was holding inside himself, something that he had not been able to speak about, had learned to believe it was wrong to speak about. Was it that he believed something else should be written? that the time for telling stories was over? that all the stories had been told? Or was it that he believed what he had been told about telling and because of that could not begin to tell?

One morning he fished the story out of his desk and began reading it. What was about someone else, someone he made up, was about him and his brother, the one hanging in chains, the one in the photographs he had been holding, the one who never answered any questions. And now they were all inside him. In the story he had written, the older brother does not return. In the story he had not written, the older brother does not lower his brother to the floor. The brother hanging from the ceiling has been writing the same story over and over, he thought. He has not found a way out of his story, has not found a way to release himself from its words, has not found a way to make the ending change. He has stayed inside the story in which he makes himself up in a room of make-believe. He is listening to himself tell a story, and he is playing all the parts. It is a story no one else, not even his brother, has heard. It is a story told to him over and over again until finally he believes there is no other story, and begins telling it to himself.

V

The brother who liked to watch a woman undress had been beaten by his father many times. How many times is too many? he thought. When is enough more than enough? How far is too far? Once, while writing a letter to his father detailing each of the times he remembered clearly, he thought he should stop because he never spent a night in the hospital. Was he, as his father insisted, stubborn? Was he, as his father had repeated, bad? The brother who wore dresses never said if he had read the letter his older brother mailed to their father, the letter their father had read to the older brother's wife. The brother who wore dresses never mentioned that his older brother's wife had come and stayed with him and their father during Christmas, and that they had all spoken of the older brother's repeated desertions. Later, on the phone, his wife would tell him that she had been surprised by the calm, matter-of-fact tone of his letter, that the father had said to her after she had read the letter that his son was very spoiled when he was young, and that he was still spoiled or he wouldn't have left her. She would ask him why he couldn't see what had happened to him from his father's point of view.

Do you or anyone else have to be there to know what actually happened? he thought. Is this what must happen for you to know what actually occurred in this room or that? The stories that never get told, the ones that each of us has kept—are these what must be secretly repeated in order for us to pass safely through each day?

He was looking at the photographs, but he was not in the room in which they were taken, basement of a suburban ranch

206

home, formica paneling, and a bleached blonde in a red leather skirt, white satin blouse, and purple sunglasses, holding a whip and smiling.

One brother knew he had been hit many times, the other brother never mentioned whether he was hit or not. One watched, the other wore. One moved from room to room, and house to house, while the other sat still or stood and waited. Neither of them spoke of that when they spoke.

Edificio Sayonara

It is time to say good-bye, adios, sayonara. He heard the words and then wrote them down. He knew what they meant but he was not sure what he meant by them. Yes, it is time to say goodbye, adios, sayonara, but he was not sure to who or what he was saying or thinking these words, or if he was saying or thinking them. It may be that these words are departing, are turning and looking back before they vanish through the door separating him from the earth.

He wondered how long he had lived above the earth, above the room he saw himself in, walking across its wooden floor to pick up a green and white book, riffle its pale pages until he found the illustration he was looking for. He wondered if the one he was looking at was him or someone that looked like him, someone who ate at the same table with someone who knew his name, the name he called himself by when he went took the bag of dirty clothes to the laundry or ordered a blender from a catalogue.

He asked her what she was doing. I am masturbating. I am lying in the dark, listening to your voice and masturbating. But I have given you a different face and body, the face and body of a lion though now that I have told you that I will change your face and body into something else, something

208

that will bring me back to the muddy field where I first met you, where we first made love, before you ever looked up from behind your desk and saw me looking back.

He heard the words and decided to write them down. The voice was his though he was not speaking. He wondered how long it had been talking and why he had not heard it before. Someday I will learn to speak, someday I will have assembled all the words I need in order to say what it is I need to say but until that time comes I will sit here and listen. He began listening to himself listen. A slight murmur, like that of distant traffic on a rainy night. moved in the distance.

Each summer his father went to Las Vegas and gambled on the shape of the future, while his mother stayed home and told him stories about her childhood—the bright colors of its passing—in a country she had no desire to return to. He thought he would someday be able to find the space between his father's schemes to control the future and his mother's memories of the past.

I would like to get married; have a child; leave the city; go on some kind of assistance so we can have more time to be with each other. But before doing that I would like to sleep with this man I met the other night, he does not look like you so that is good. We might all be together one day, but I would not want to be the center of attention. I want something else but not right now or maybe now but not the now we are in but the one we are about to be in, the one that is coming towards us. Right now, I need some stability. I need to see you sitting there. I need to know you will be alone in that chair when I come back from the store.

His parents had traveled a long distance to come to America. They once lived in different parts of a city that no longer existed, its name assigned to either the cold pages of history books or the yellowed pages of novels in which passion tore the characters into tiny pieces for others to scoop up while they walked toward the temple in the mountains.

He used to tie me to the bed before he went out. Sometimes he would be gone all afternoon. He once told me he had murdered a man and buried him in the field near our house. He said no one missed him and no one would ever find him. He said that he loved me. He said that I had to learn that this was how it was done.

I have to count all the windows. I will only live in a house that has an odd number of windows, thirteen or seventeen, say. I only wear brown or green. Blue reminds me of the sky or the ocean. I will not wear blue. I will not eat off blue dishes or drink out of blue cups. I will not allow my body to merge with anything but the earth.

He had been masturbating in front of a mirror, seeing if he could change his face into someone else's when he heard a door open and a voice he did not know call out his name.

He had a thought. It was not his. He put it out of his mind, onto the table, next to the blue vase containing yellow flowers. The thought returned to its cage and sang. He listened to its melody. In a few months or years he would learn the meaning of its song.

Printed November 1992 in Santa Barbara & Ann
Arbor for the Black Sparrow Press by Mackintosh
Typography & Edwards Brothers Inc. Text set in
Galliard by Words Worth. Design by Barbara Martin.
This edition is published in paper wrappers;
there are 200 hardcover trade copies;
125 hardcover copies have been numbered & signed
by the author; & 26 copies handbound in boards
by Earle Gray are lettered & signed by the author.

Photo: Peter Muscato

John Yau was born in Lynn, Massachusetts in 1950, and was educated at Bard College (B.A. 1972) and Brooklyn College (M.F.A. 1977). An independent art critic since 1978, he has written for well-known American and European publications, including *Art in America, Artforum, Art News, Arts, Art Space, Flash Art, Interview, Tema Celeste,* and *Vogue,* as well as contributed more than a hundred essays and introductions to monographs and exhibition catalogs of contemporary art and artists such as Anna Bialobroda, Jasper Johns, Joan Mitchell, Bruce Nauman, Miguel Angel Rios, and Jackie Winsor.

He has taught at Bard College (Milton Avery Graduate School of the Arts), Brooklyn College, Emerson College, Maryland Institute College of Art, Poetry Project (St. Mark's Church), Pratt Institute, School of Visual Arts, and in the Creative Writing Department at Brown University (Spring '92).

A recipient of fellowships from the National Endowment for the Arts, the Ingram-Merrill Foundation, and the New York Foundation of the Arts, he was awarded a General Electric Foundation Award and the Lavan Award (Academy of American Poets) in 1988. His books include *Broken Off by the Music, Corpse and Mirror,* which was chosen by John Ashbery to appear in the National Poetry Series, and *Radiant Silhouette: New & Selected Work 1974–1988. Big City Primer: Reading New York at the End of the Twentieth Century*—a collaboration with the artist Bill Barrette—was published in 1991, and received the Brendan Gill Award.

His essay, "Famous Paintings Seen, Not Looked At, Not Examined," will be included in *Hand-Painted Pop,* and a monograph on the contemporary German artist A.R. Penck is forthcoming. He is currently working on a book about Jasper Johns, a "notebook" about Andy Warhol, as well as collaborating with the artist Bill Barrette on a second book of poems and photographs, this one about Berlin. He lives and works in New York City.